"There could not be a more important time to be considering the role of philanthropy in society. This book brilliantly and intelligently places contemporary debates in a historic context. In doing so, Rhodri Davies avoids the extremes of being simply a cheerleader on the one hand, or undertaking a hatchet job on the other. Essential reading for anyone interested in the charity sector."
Paul Ramsbottom OBE, Chief Executive, Wolfson Foundation

"An unbiased analysis of the various approaches our sector engages in – equal parts historic treatise and futurism think-piece, which tries to answer the salient question: how can we improve philanthropy?"
Edgar Villanueva, activist, author and founder/principal of Decolonizing Wealth Project and Liberated Capital

"An indispensable, eminently readable guide to philanthropy's relationship to democracy, the state and social ethics, brimming with insights and alive to its complexities."
Benjamin Soskis, The Urban Institute

The status quo is broken. Humanity today faces multiple interconnected challenges, some of which could prove existential. If we believe the world could be different, if we want it to be *better*, examining the purpose of what we do – and what is done in our name – is more pressing than ever.

The What Is It For? series examines the purpose of the most important aspects of our contemporary world, from religion and free speech to animal rights and the Olympics. It illuminates what these things are by looking closely at what they do.

The series offers fresh thinking on current debates that gets beyond the overheated polemics and easy polarizations. Across the series, leading experts explore new ways forward, enabling readers to engage with the possibility of real change.

Series editor: George Miller

Visit **bristoluniversitypress.co.uk/whats-it-for**
to find out more about the series.

RHODRI DAVIES is the founding Director of the think tank Why Philanthropy Matters, and a Pears Research Fellow at the Centre for Philanthropy, University of Kent. He is also the host of the Philanthropisms podcast. Until September 2021 he was Head of Policy at the Charities Aid Foundation (CAF), where he led Giving Thought, an in-house think tank focusing on philanthropy and civil society issues.

WHAT IS PHILANTHROPY FOR?

RHODRI DAVIES

First published in Great Britain in 2023 by

Bristol University Press
University of Bristol
1–9 Old Park Hill
Bristol
BS2 8BB
UK
t: +44 (0)117 374 6645
e: bup-info@bristol.ac.uk

Details of international sales and distribution partners are available at
bristoluniversitypress.co.uk

British Library Cataloguing in Publication Data
A catalogue record for this book is available from the British Library

ISBN 978-1-5292-2692-8 paperback
ISBN 978-1-5292-2693-5 ePub
ISBN 978-1-5292-2694-2 ePdf

Cover design: Tom Appshaw

To Fran, Elsa and Martha: thank you for inspiring me, putting up with me and making me proud and happy pretty much every day. I love you all, and I promise to write a murder mystery next time.

CONTENTS

LIST OF FIGURES, TABLES AND BOXES

Figures

Tables

Boxes

1
INTRODUCTION

Philanthropy means different things to different people. Some use the word almost exclusively to talk about extravagant acts of generosity by the very rich, while others argue it's more about valuing modest acts of everyday kindness across society. Critics dismiss philanthropy as vanity projects for billionaires; supporters cite its long track record of promoting social progress and innovation.

Whatever the interpretation, philanthropy is often portrayed as a niche issue, just a curious footnote in mainstream political debate. But this perception could not be more wrong. As you'll discover in this book, philanthropy has for centuries played a major role in shaping our world, from sustaining the anti-slavery movement to supporting cutting-edge medical research. At micro level, it reflects fundamental truths about the values we hold and how we interact with one another, so questions that are seemingly about philanthropy often lead to far deeper ethical or moral considerations.

At macro level, philanthropy is a vital mechanism for redistributing resources within society alongside the state and the market, so questions about philanthropy become political questions about liberty, justice and what we want our society to look like.

Given the variations in how philanthropy is defined and measured across countries, it is impossible to calculate a credible figure for its total global value. However, we know that individuals in the UK gave £11.3 billion in 2021[1] and that in the US they gave a near-record $485 billion in the same year.[2] A 2018 Harvard University report estimated that the total value of assets in philanthropic foundations across twenty-three countries was $1.5 trillion,[3] and the Organization for Economic Co-operation and Development (OECD) estimates that around $10.6 billion of private philanthropy goes towards development around the globe each year.[4] In the context of governmental spending these figures may not be huge (the OECD notes that although philanthropic funding for development totalled $42.5 billion between 2016 and 2019, official development assistance (ODA) in the same period was more than ten times as much ($595.5 billion)). But philanthropic capital is often targeted in ways that have far greater impact than straightforward dollar amounts might suggest. As such, this is a subject that both deserves and demands our attention.

To add further urgency, philanthropy is at a turning point. Recent years have seen a high-profile wave of criticism levelled at the idea of people using private

Table 1.1: The ten largest philanthropic foundations in the world[5]

Name	Country of origin	Founded	Original source of wealth	Endowed assets (USD billion)
Novo Nordisk Foundation	Denmark	1989	Corporate shareholding in pharmaceutical companies (Novo Nordisk and Novozymes)	69.6
Bill & Melinda Gates Foundation	USA	1994	Personal wealth of Bill & Melinda Gates, corporate shareholdings	51.9
Stichting INGKA Foundation	Netherlands	1982	Personal wealth of Ingvar Kamprad (founder of IKEA), ownership of INGKA Holdings	38.8
Wellcome Trust	UK	1936	Legacy bequest from pharmaceutical millionaire Henry Wellcome	37
Mastercard Foundation	Canada	2006	Shares created during 2006 Initial Public Offering (IPO)	31.5
Howard Hughes Medical Institute	USA	1953	Shareholding (100 per cent) in Hughes Aircraft	27.1
Azim Premji Foundation	India	2001	Personal wealth of Wipro CEO Azim Premji	21
Open Society Foundations	USA	1993	Personal wealth of investor George Soros	19.6

(continued)

Table 1.1: The ten largest philanthropic foundations in the world (continued)

Name	Country of origin	Founded	Original source of wealth	Endowed assets (USD billion)
Lilly Endowment	USA	1937	Personal wealth of Josiah K. Lilly Sr and his sons, Eli Jr and Josiah Jr, shareholdings in Eli Lilly & Co.	15.1
Ford Foundation	USA	1936	Personal wealth of Edsel and Henry Ford; shareholdings in Ford Motor Company	13.7

Figure 1.1: Priorities of philanthropic foundations[6]

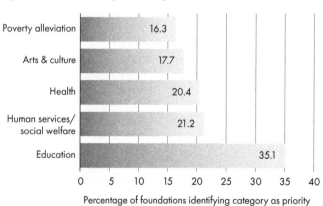

Percentage of foundations identifying category as priority

assets for the public good. Some critics argue that philanthropy only exists because wealth is so unevenly distributed, so it is a *symptom* of inequality, not part of the cure. Others claim that by giving those with financial resources a means to influence public policy and debate outside the electoral system, philanthropy is inherently anti-democratic. The COVID-19 pandemic has amplified many of these concerns over inequality and accountability, leading some critics to conclude that philanthropy needs to be fundamentally reshaped if it is to play a positive role in our future.

The context in which philanthropy operates is also changing rapidly. The landscape for 'doing good' is expanding as new opportunities emerge for people to dedicate their time and resources to causes they care about. Traditional charitable organizations increasingly find themselves competing with alternatives such as crowdfunding, impact investing (combining for-profit financial approaches with a social goal) and online social movements. Meanwhile, societal expectations about the relative roles of philanthropy, the state and the market are evolving. The COVID-19 pandemic gave many of us a greater appreciation than ever before of the need for action by the state, yet conversely has highlighted the vital roles that philanthropy can fulfil, as donors played a part in everything from providing direct support for foodbanks and frontline healthcare to funding the development and rollout of vaccine programmes. The pandemic has also furthered a trend for businesses to claim a 'social purpose' and thus encroach on territory that would once have been seen as the preserve of charities. This raises fundamental questions about what, if anything, is the unique contribution of philanthropy to society today.

As we look to the future, it pays to look back at the past. Although history is not an infallible guide, understanding the historical development of philanthropy illuminates why we have the institutions and norms we have today. It can also provide a rich domain of possibilities for thinking about what the future could be. Yet the history of philanthropy remains under-studied by academics and poorly understood by practitioners (and everyone else). This book will therefore highlight many examples where historical understanding can inform and enrich current debates about philanthropy and give us new insights about how it could develop in the future.

What *is* philanthropy?

Having made a case that philanthropy is worth our attention, there is another even more basic question we need to address before we dig into its purpose: namely, what *is* philanthropy? This seems like a straightforward matter of definitions – particularly for a word we are going to be using freely throughout this book – but it is remarkably difficult to answer this question with any precision.

Etymologically, we are on firm enough ground: any book about philanthropy you pick up will tell you the word's roots are in ancient Greek and that it means 'love of humanity'. We can even identify a first usage:

in the fifth century BCE play *Prometheus Unbound*, Aeschylus described Prometheus as a 'philanthropist' for daring to steal the secret of fire from the Gods and give it to humans. However, this doesn't tell us much about how the word is used today, or indeed, the many different ways in which it has been used in the intervening 2,500 years.

Understanding the historical development of philanthropy from its roots in the classical world to the present day is hugely valuable as a way of unpacking the modern meaning of the word and unpicking its nuances and complexities, and this book will lean heavily on historical insight as a tool for understanding philanthropy today. However, knowledge of history is not by itself enough to give us a firm definition of philanthropy. And maybe we should not even be looking for that. Perhaps such a definition does not exist, so our starting point needs to be acceptance of this fact rather than searching in vain for consensus on its precise meaning.

To get a sense of why this might be the case, consider the various ways we might try to draw boundaries around the usage of 'philanthropy'. Is it, for instance, to do with amounts? Is philanthropy about rich people giving away large sums of money? This certainly seems to chime with the fact that 'philanthropy' is often used to talk about the giving of the super-rich. It quickly becomes clear, though, that this fails as a definition. For one thing, there are plenty who reject any implied link between philanthropy and wealth; there is a growing chorus of people right now arguing that we actively need to reclaim the word philanthropy from any such associations, as they exclude the many acts of generosity that people of more modest means do every day.

Even if we did think 'philanthropy' referred to larger acts of giving, where would we draw the line? Would there be a point at which a gift of X pounds or dollars was seen as a 'mere act of charity', while a gift of X+1 qualified as philanthropy? Some would also argue that giving is only meaningful if it comes with an element of sacrifice; hence the old Yiddish saying that 'if charity cost no money and benevolence caused no heartache, the world would be full of philanthropists'. Since what counts as a genuine sacrifice is clearly dependent on how much you have in the first place, would the threshold for a gift to count as philanthropy therefore need to be proportional to the wealth of the giver?

Perhaps the distinguishing characteristic of philanthropy is not the amount, but the *manner* of giving? Maybe we need to stipulate, for instance, that we are talking only about gifts of financial resources. But again, this doesn't really work – it's too narrow. There is a well-worn saying in the philanthropy world that we need to think about 'the three Ts': time, talent and treasure. This means taking into account the volunteer work people do and the skills they dedicate to charitable projects just as much as the money they contribute. We also need to consider whether our definitions over-emphasize formal methods of giving (such as donations or volunteering done through registered charities or nonprofit organizations) at the expense of the vast range of informal methods that often pass under the radar of both historical records and current approaches to measurement. Given that these informal methods have often, by necessity, been vital to those who are excluded from mainstream charity (such as the working class in the nineteenth century or minority communities today), failing to include them in our definition of philanthropy risks perpetuating the cycle of exclusion.

Some might argue that we need to define philanthropy by the *what*: by the kinds of causes and activities support is directed towards. It is certainly true that most countries define in law the range of causes that count as charitable and the activities that are legitimate in pursuit of them. However, it is far from clear that we would want our overall concept of philanthropy to be dictated by them, as that would give the government the power to define philanthropy. This is problematic in theoretical terms, since we surely want philanthropy to be independent of direct government control. It is also problematic in practical terms, as controlling what counts as philanthropy is a tool for governments to constrain the rights and freedoms of civil society, as many have already chosen to do.

It is also true that one of the common distinctions drawn by people trying to define philanthropy is between activity focused on addressing the *symptoms* of problems and activity that aims to get at their underlying *causes*. The former, it's claimed, is the domain of charity, while the latter is the focus of philanthropy. Again, there is something in this: it is certainly true that plenty of what we would consider as textbook examples of philanthropy throughout history have focused on campaigning and advocacy designed to drive changes in public opinion or the law at least as much as they have on delivering direct services to those in need. So it is crucial that any definition of philanthropy we put forward can encompass this kind of campaigning. But it is also clear that we cannot restrict our definition *only* to this kind of activity, as far from all philanthropy takes this form; direct service provision remains a key element of many approaches.

Finally, can we define philanthropy by the *why*? Is an understanding of people's motivations enough to class their actions as philanthropy? This certainly seems to work in the negative, as often the basis for claiming that an apparent act of generosity should *not* be classified as philanthropy is questioning the donor's motivation, for example, by arguing that they are driven more by ego or reputational gain, and a desire to have their name in large letters on a building, than by genuine charity or altruism. The problem, of course, is that we can never really know what is in another person's heart, so any ascription of motivation for giving must be based either on our own assessment or on other people's claims. The former, however, is only ever really a reflection of our existing view of the person (shaped by our assumptions and biases), while the latter should be subject to the same scepticism we would level at any self-report of motive (people are generally bad at identifying their own reasons for acting and often have an incentive to misrepresent their true motives).

This may all be irrelevant in any case, as some would rule out motivation as a criterion for identifying philanthropy. The philanthropy scholar Dwight Burlinghame, for instance, has argued that 'altruism is not the single motive for defining philanthropy, nor is it necessarily the desired operational motive'.[7] If this is true then all that matters is *how* someone is giving, not *why* they are doing so (which brings us back to where we started).

Defining philanthropy is clearly difficult, but that does not mean we have to give up. For one thing, there are definitions which, although not perfect, do a pretty good job of capturing large parts of what we might want to convey. Philanthropy scholar Robert Payton's pithy rendering of philanthropy as 'voluntary action for the public good' is perhaps the most widely cited.[8] In addition, maybe we just need to embrace the fuzziness of the concept. Many scholars now agree that philanthropy is best understood as an 'essentially contested term', whose definition is inherently subject to debate, or as an 'umbrella term' under which a diverse array of topics fall (some of which may be conflicting or contradictory). The US Supreme Court Justice Potter Stewart famously said in a 1964 obscenity trial that 'hardcore pornography' is not something that can be readily defined but 'I know it when I see it', and perhaps philanthropy is similarly something that we need to accept that we know when we see.

There is, however, a further option: even if we cannot specify exactly what philanthropy is, we might be able to bring it into sharper relief by exploring what it *isn't*. Think of this like delineating the borders of a country by tracing where they meet its neighbours, even if those borders are sometimes unclear or disputed. And that is the approach this book will take: each chapter is framed as a debate between philanthropy and something that it is not, but which it is commonly compared to. So we will consider how philanthropy relates to charity, justice, the state, democracy and the market. Exploring the points of similarity and difference with each of these will bring to light important aspects of the nature of philanthropy and help us to understand the major debates and themes that have shaped giving throughout history. This will enable us to determine what philanthropy is for today – and also point us towards how it needs to change to meet the needs of the future.

2
PHILANTHROPY OR CHARITY?

'The difference between charity and philanthropy', declared a Welsh newspaper in 1905, 'is that philanthropy can afford to engage a press agent.'[1] This is clearly flippant, but it does highlight the fact that comparisons with charity have long been central to discussions of philanthropy, stretching back hundreds of years. This distinction continues to play a big part in shaping views and approaches even today, so unpicking how and why it has been drawn is crucial for our efforts to determine what philanthropy is for.

Religious charity vs secular philanthropy?

One way of distinguishing between charity and philanthropy, some people would argue, is that the former is inherently religious and the latter secular. There is something in this, as religion has certainly been an important factor in shaping the historical relationship between these two ideas. However, philanthropy is not simply charity's secular cousin. For one thing, this fails to capture many of the other aspects of the difference; and for another, it doesn't reflect the reality of how we understand charity and philanthropy today. Many of us give to charity for reasons that have nothing to do with religion and in doing so support organizations that are entirely secular. (Although it should be noted that religious causes still get the largest share of all charitable giving in both the UK and US – around 17 per cent in the former and roughly one-third in the latter – and that religiosity also plays a major role in the cultures of giving of many other countries around the world.)[2] So charity cannot be said to be *inherently* religious. Conversely, many philanthropists give for religious reasons or to causes and organizations that are to some extent religious, so philanthropy cannot be thought of as wholly secular either.

It is certainly true that the word 'philanthropy' has secular roots. We have already seen that it first appeared in ancient Greece, where *philanthropia* referred to a broad concept of civic virtue. Giving was often a part of this, but it was by no means the most important part. And where gifts were made, they were not motivated by pity for the poor or designed to alleviate the suffering of particular individuals, but rather were public in nature: gifts to the populace as a whole motivated by a sense of good citizenship and duty. 'Charity', on the other hand, has its roots in religion. Although the word comes from the Latin *caritas* (albeit via a circuitous route), it was through its adoption in the Christian tradition that it really came to prominence, denoting a virtue of mercy and care for the suffering of individual fellow humans that was sanctified by the church and supposed to reflect the grace of God. As Christianity spread throughout the Western world, the ascent of 'charity' was matched by the decline of 'philanthropy', to the extent that it largely disappeared from the lexicon – certainly in English – for the best part of a millennium.

Christian ideas of charity were dominant in Europe throughout the medieval period. These are often depicted in modern accounts as revolving solely around almsgiving: gifts from the rich to the poor, administered by the church and motivated by the promise of securing entry to heaven for those deemed sufficiently generous. A crucial feature of such almsgiving is that it is usually taken to be solely about the intention of the giver, not the worth of the recipient or effectiveness of the gift, although many scholars have pointed out that this is something of a caricature and that we should be careful about making any assumption that medieval notions of charity were simple or uniform.

In any case, by the sixteenth century those ideas were about to get shaken up in a big way (along with many other things) by the Reformation. This marked an important turning point in the development of philanthropy because, argues the historian W.K. Jordan, the desire of Protestants to ensure that anything Catholic was seen as backward and bad meant that 'such men scorned and disdained alms, the mechanism of mediaeval charity, since they were profoundly persuaded that casual, undisciplined charity was as ineffective as it was wasteful.'[3] As such, giving and the proper way to do it became an important part of the propaganda war between Protestants and Catholics. The poet John Donne (a Protestant convert) boldly asserted that: 'There have been in this kingdome, since the blessed reformation of religion, more publick charitable works perform'd, more hospitals and colleges erected and endowed in threescore, than in some hundreds of years of superstition before.'[4] And he was far from alone in this kind of rhetoric.

The Reformation was important in laying the foundations for a shift toward a new conception of charity in which, according to the scholar Gareth Jones, 'the objects of charity became more secular as the majority of Englishmen reflected less on the fate of their souls and became more concerned with the worldly needs of their fellow men.'[5] However, it is by no means the only explanation for the secularization of charity that took place from the sixteenth century; a similar process was happening across continental Europe, including in countries that remained resolutely Catholic. Just as important was the rise of a new form of secular humanism, led by thinkers such as the Catholic Dutch scholar Erasmus. Then, during the Enlightenment in the eighteenth century, revolutionary new ideas about God, reason, nature and humanity caused seismic shifts in art, science, philosophy and politics. This included major changes in how people thought about the nature of poverty and the role of charity. Poverty was no longer something that had to be accepted (or even welcomed) as a necessary part of how God had ordered the world; but was instead now seen as a societal flaw that could be addressed. Charity might have a role in this, but it was not the only option; where it failed to address issues at the required structural level it should be replaced, many thinkers now argued, by taxation and other state mechanisms.

It was one of the main forerunners of the Enlightenment, Sir Francis Bacon, who gets the credit for reintroducing the concept of philanthropy to English readers in 1612, though he stuck to the Greek form *philanthropia* and was careful to stress that it was

Figure 2.1: John Howard, from *Anecdotes of the life and character of John Howard, Esq.*, 1790

John Howard was the first person described as a philanthropist in the modern sense of the word. A prison reformer whose tireless efforts to document the appalling conditions in prisons throughout Britain and Europe earned him widespread admiration during his lifetime, Howard became even more famous after his death and was often cited as the archetype of an ideal philanthropist well into the nineteenth century.

an ancient Greek concept that didn't really have any direct translation into English.[6] As the word made its home once again in the English language, however, it developed new associations. At first these were primarily with social and political campaigning (the eighteenth-century English prison reformer John Howard, for example, is widely acknowledged as the first person to be labelled a philanthropist in our modern sense).[7] Then, as the eighteenth and nineteenth centuries wore on and new forms of voluntary association 'came to luxurious bloom' (as David Owen memorably put it),[8] philanthropy was increasingly associated with the idea of donating money to charitable institutions. Finally, the arrival of the twentieth century saw the growth of vast fortunes among the industrialist titans of the United States, many of whom began to put those fortunes towards philanthropy (in part, one suspects, in the hope of rebalancing their reputations as 'robber barons'). Figures such as Andrew Carnegie and John D. Rockefeller institutionalized their generosity in huge charitable foundations and in doing so established a new template for philanthropy, one that echoes to this day, since for many people philanthropy still suggests large fortunes and something distinctly American (even if, as we have seen, this couldn't be further from the truth, historically speaking).

Tackling root causes or symptoms?

It is clear that an important point of difference between philanthropy and charity is that the former was taken to be at least partly secular. However, that is not enough to explain the distinction fully. For proponents of philanthropy, its defining characteristic was not simply that it was not based in religion, but that it differed from religious models in being universal (rather than individual) in scope and at the same time discriminating (rather than universal) in application. Charity, it was claimed, at best ameliorated the symptoms of society's problems by providing direct help to individuals; philanthropy, meanwhile, sought to address the root causes of those problems as well. As the historian Robert Gross writes in tracing the development of distinct notions of charity and philanthropy in the US:

> Charity engages individuals in concrete, direct acts of compassion and connection to other people ... [Philanthropy] aspires not so much to aid individuals as to reform society. By eliminating the problems of society that beset particular persons, philanthropy aims to usher in a world where charity is uncommon – and perhaps unnecessary.[9]

The idea that societal problems such as poverty could be 'solved' by philanthropy represented a radical shift in thinking. The medieval notion of poverty, typified by the writings of Thomas Aquinas, was that it reflected God's design: some people were poor while others were rich, and that was just how things were. The poor could take comfort in knowing they were closer to God, since poverty was a virtue; meanwhile the rich had a duty to offload the spiritual burden that came with wealth by giving alms to the poor. There was no

Figure 2.2: Portrait of Andrew Carnegie, by unidentified artist, oil on canvas, c. 1905

Scottish-American steel magnate Andrew Carnegie came from humble beginnings to become one of the dominant philanthropic figures of the early twentieth century. His approach to giving, with a strong emphasis on 'scientific' methods and avoiding 'indiscriminate charity' at all costs, was outlined in his 1889 essay 'The Gospel of Wealth', which continues to be highly influential to this day.

suggestion, however, that the purpose of giving was to alter this order. It was only during the Enlightenment, which brought radical new political and economic ideas, that philosophers started to think of poverty as a systemic failing of society that could potentially be corrected rather than an unavoidable fact. From the late seventeenth century this also led to the idea that philanthropy, if done properly, could remove the need for charity altogether. This is a view still heard today: in 2009, for instance, the President of the Carnegie Corporation, Vartan Gregorian, declared that 'philanthropy works to do away with the causes that necessitate charity'.[10]

Criticism of universal philanthropy

When presented simply in terms of a focus on root causes rather than symptoms, it might seem obvious that philanthropy is an improvement on charity. However, in practice philanthropy has often been criticized by those who feel that in striving to be universal and rational, it too often becomes cold and impersonal, and loses sight of the basic human attributes of kindness and care for one's neighbour embodied in acts of charity. The stereotype of the pompous and disagreeable 'do-gooder' was in fact a staple of satire from the eighteenth century onwards. W.S. Gilbert (of Gilbert and Sullivan fame) captured one aspect of this stereotype in a verse entitled 'The Disagreeable Man', which paints a vivid picture of a priggish individual whose approach alienates all around him:

If you give me your attention, I will tell you what I am:
I'm a genuine philanthropist – all other kinds are sham.
Each little fault of temper and each social defect
In my erring fellow creatures, I endeavour to correct.[11]

Part of the problem, declared an article in *The Times* in 1914, is that 'the philanthropist often seems to overlook the individual in his passion for the general' and this tends to happen both because 'concrete men persist in treating him just as if he were one of themselves' rather than acknowledging his special status and because real people are frustratingly fallible and thus 'fall short of his conception of what man ought to be'.[12] The temptation, therefore, is to retreat into abstract philanthropy that deals only with the world as it should be, rather than as it is.

Critics have also argued that the universal aspirations of philanthropy, unlike charity, can lead to a preference for grand schemes and utopian visions over the basic hard work of helping people in immediate need. Some have argued these schemes can directly lead to harm, if those who design them become so caught up in their plans that they lose sight of their real-world impacts. The most famous satirical take on this is probably Jonathan Swift's *A Modest Proposal*, in which he argues that the solution to the problem of child poverty is to encourage 'philanthropic cannibalism', in other words, parents should eat children they are unable to care for.[13] Clearly this is horrifying in itself, but what is more horrifying is how rational Swift manages to make it seem as a solution to the problem – and in doing so he provides a highly effective satire of the kinds of utopian philanthropic schemes that were rife in the eighteenth century.

More commonly, however, the thrust of satirical attacks on the grand visions of philanthropy has been that, while not necessarily harmful in themselves, they do harm by distracting attention from more prosaic

Figure 2.3: 'The Universal Philanthropist'. Process print after G. Cruikshank, 1848

This cartoon by famed illustrator George Cruikshank shows a man kicking out at a starving family who have asked him for help. He is angry at them for interrupting him when he is 'perfecting a grand benevolent plan of universal brotherhood'. It deftly captures the long-standing critique that elaborate, top-down philanthropy can too often get in the way of basic human charity and kindness.

and immediate needs. The famed illustrator George Cruikshank deftly skewered philanthropy's occasional tendency to focus on grandiose schemes in a cartoon of 1848 entitled 'The Universal Philanthropist', which depicts a well-dressed gentleman aiming a kick at a poor family, who cower to get out of his way. The father of the poor family is saying, 'Please Sir, bestow your charity for we are starving!', to which the philanthropist angrily responds, 'Interrupting me … at a moment when I am perfecting a grand benevolent plan of Universal Brotherhood and Community of Goods, for the amelioration of the whole Human Race!

Why, you ungrateful wretch, get out of my house and learn to love your benefactors!'[14]

'Telescopic philanthropy'

A criticism that became particularly widespread in the nineteenth century was that philanthropists' desire to act universally led them to focus on issues overseas at the expense of more immediate needs at home. As George Eliot notes in *Middlemarch* (1871), 'we all know the wag's definition of a philanthropist: a man whose charity increases directly as the square of the distance'. This was often disparagingly dubbed 'telescopic philanthropy', as captured in a famous 1865 *Punch* cartoon.[15] Here the figure of Britannia looks out to sea through a telescope while a group of poor urchins grab at her robes and ask, 'Please Madam, ain't we black enough to be cared for?' As this clearly demonstrates, the critique of telescopic philanthropy had its roots in well-worn arguments about 'charity beginning at home', but was also inextricably tied up with nationalism and xenophobia, and as such often used racialized imagery and language that is deeply uncomfortable to modern eyes.

One of the notable early critiques of telescopic philanthropy came from British statesman George Canning (who, until the recent brief tenure of Liz Truss, held the record as Britain's shortest-serving prime minister). Canning was a nationalist and a fervent opponent of Jacobinism and the ideals of the French Revolution; in 1798 he published a satirical poem entitled 'New Morality' in which he lambasted what he saw as the vile threat of 'French' (by which he meant universalist) philanthropy:

First, stern PHILANTHROPY: —not she, who dries
The orphan's tears, and wipes the widow's eyes;
Not she, who sainted Charity her guide,
Of British bounty pours the annual tide:
But French PHILANTHROPY;—whose boundless mind
Glows with the general love of all mankind.[16]

The Victorian era saw Britain's empire at its height, so thoughts of far-flung possessions and dominions, and the responsibilities they brought, were never far from the nation's mind. Unsurprisingly, attacks on telescopic philanthropy also reached their peak in this period. Charles Dickens immortalized the idea in the character of Mrs Jellyby in *Bleak House*, whose zeal for supporting missionary work and philanthropic projects in Africa leads her to neglect her family and let her own children go hungry. *The Times*, meanwhile, was staunchly critical of telescopic philanthropy throughout the nineteenth century. In 1840 it reprinted a poem from the satirical magazine *John Bull* entitled 'Ode to Modern Philanthropy', which mocked what it saw as the failure of anti-slavery campaigners to start their charity at home:

Your thorough-bred philanthropists can glance
Their pitying eyes over Earth's expanse,
Til sorrow all their bosoms discomposes

For their black brethren sold to whips and chains;
And not a single sympathy remain
For starving whites who die beneath their noses.[17]

The overt racism on display in many examples of the telescopic philanthropy critique is likely to strike us these days as abhorrent. But just as uncomfortable is the suspicion that as a society we have not entirely put such attitudes behind us. In 2021 the UK's national lifeboat charity, the RNLI, was the subject of a concerted hate campaign led by a far-right group incensed by the charity's rescue of 'foreigners' crossing the English Channel in often highly perilous conditions to seek refuge or asylum in Britain. Likewise, researchers in the US have found that some people are less likely to give to a charity when it supports immigrants, especially if they are undocumented.[18] Many of the attacks on international aid and development in recent years are underpinned by a nationalist mindset and justified by appeal to the same notions of 'charity beginning at home' that gave rise to critiques of telescopic philanthropy for so long.

Rational and discriminating?

Philanthropy's focus on addressing causes rather than symptoms is sometimes reflected in methods and approaches that are entirely distinct from those of charity, but not always. When dealing with issues of poverty, for instance, there is always likely to be some element of direct distribution of resources in the form of grants or cash gifts that looks (on the surface at least) very much like charitable efforts in the same field. How then does philanthropy try to distinguish itself from charity in these instances? The answer hinges on the notions of rationality and discrimination. Charity, it is argued (usually by its critics), is driven by the heart, so resources are given out unquestioningly to all and guided only by emotion or religious duty. Philanthropy, on the other hand, is a matter of the head: resources are distributed in a rational way that accords with some theory about how best to achieve the desired end. In practice, this has often manifested in distinctions between the 'deserving' and 'undeserving' poor, and efforts to find ways of helping the former while avoiding giving to the latter at all costs.

The fear of 'indiscriminate giving' has haunted philanthropy for hundreds of years. Scottish–American industrialist and philanthropist Andrew Carnegie claimed in 1906 that 'one of the serious obstacles to the improvement of our race is indiscriminate charity', and that 'of every thousand dollars spent in so-called charity today … it is probable that $950 is unwisely spent; so spent, indeed as to produce the very evils which it proposes to mitigate or cure.'[19] It was a common refrain: indiscriminate giving was not merely wasteful but actively detrimental because it bred dependency and encouraged laziness on the part of the poor. Over a century before Carnegie, the writer Dr Samuel Johnson argued that 'you do more good to [the poor] by spending [money] in luxury than by giving it; for by spending it in luxury you make them exert industry, whereas by giving it, you keep them idle.'[20] Some even argued that ill-considered charity was the main problem in society; the Victorian economist William Stanley Jevons, for instance, claimed that 'much of the poverty and crime which now exist have been caused by mistaken charity in past times.'[21]

The introduction of Poor Law legislation in many European countries, beginning in the pre-industrial era, saw the establishment of new mechanisms of government-controlled poverty relief and brought even more focus on the distinction between the deserving and the undeserving poor. The state now accepted, for the first time in many cases, some responsibility for the welfare of its citizens, a responsibility which had previously rested with the family or the church. As this required the introduction of local levies to pay for any welfare needs, all citizens now had a stake as taxpayers, which meant that many were keen to ensure that their money was 'well spent' and did not go to 'the wrong people' (concerns which still shape discussion of taxation and welfare today). Since the continuing encouragement of charitable giving to meet welfare needs was a key policy tool for local and national governments keen to minimize the need to impose deeply unpopular taxes, there was now an even greater emphasis on ensuring that giving was suitably discriminating. In England, the introduction of Poor Law legislation in 1598 was swiftly followed by the introduction of the Statute of Charitable Uses in 1601 – legislation whose primary aim was to make charitable endowments more effective while also directing them towards causes that were in line with the government's own policy priorities, so that the burden of state responsibility for welfare could be lessened. As historian Paul Slack argues, 'the poor law set out to reform and remodel charity. It should be purposive and discriminatory. Begging and casual almsgiving were to be abolished. The generous instincts of donors should be disciplined by attention to the recipients.'[22] This desire to tame the raw kindness of individuals even led the city of Hamburg to introduce a new ordinance in 1788 that made spontaneous or indiscriminate giving illegal and punishable by a fine![23]

The practical challenges of giving in a suitably discriminating way were made harder by urbanization and industrialization from the eighteenth century onwards. As populations shifted from rural areas into rapidly growing towns and cities to find work in new factories and mills, the nature and scale of issues of poverty, disease and ill health changed too. New methods of charity were needed since, according to David Owen, 'it was out of the question for the philanthropist, however well disposed, to seek out the cases of greatest need and become familiar with them … [T]o translate the person-to-person charity from the village or the small town to an urban slum was an impossible task.'[24] One result of this was the growth of 'associated philanthropy', modelled on the new joint-stock corporations that also emerged in the eighteenth century, in which donors could come together to pool resources and draw in additional expertise to ensure money was wisely distributed. This effectively marked the birth of the voluntary organization as we know it today, and the model proliferated rapidly.

The development of voluntary associations to help donors manage their giving was not, however, enough to assuage all concerns. As the nineteenth century wore on, criticisms of indiscriminate giving only grew louder and culminated in the creation in 1869 of the Charity Organization Society (COS). The COS's mission was to challenge perceived laxity and inefficiency in charitable giving and Poor Law administration, and thus to put the relief of poverty on a more 'scientific' footing. It pursued this crusade with a religious zeal and in doing so made many enemies due to its tendency to single out individual charities and philanthropists for harsh criticism, and its uncompromising dismissal of anyone who did not agree with its principles and methods. The COS also had many supporters, however – including notable philanthropists such as Octavia Hill and William Rathbone VI – and its reach spread throughout the late nineteenth and early twentieth centuries with the creation of many local chapters across the UK and beyond. The movement had a particularly notable impact in the US, as the ideas of charity organization (and what became known as 'scientific philanthropy') heavily influenced the thinking of some of the biggest philanthropists of all time. For men like John D. Rockefeller and Andrew Carnegie, the challenge of giving away large sums of money in a way that they considered effective was almost paralysing; hence Carnegie's famous declaration that 'it is more difficult to give money away intelligently than to earn it in the first place'.[25] Scientific philanthropy provided both men (and many of their contemporaries) with a framework for giving large amounts in a systematic fashion (while also justifying an emphasis on individual responsibility and self-reliance that fitted conveniently with their existing views about wealth and society).

Figure 2.4: 'Helping In/Helping Out'. Pair of cartoons from the annual report of Minneapolis Associated Charities, 1911

Helping In　　　　Helping Out

This pair of cartoons contrasts 'individual' charity with 'scientific' charity organization. The former, it is suggested, deals only with the symptoms of poverty, while the latter addresses its underlying causes by fostering self-help and social mobility, thus offering a more effective long-term solution. Advocates for 'scientific' philanthropy and defenders of individual charity clashed throughout the nineteenth and early twentieth centuries, and similar debates still shape approaches to giving today.

There were many who viewed the rise of scientific philanthropy with alarm and disdain, seeing its focus on discrimination as cruel and dehumanizing. These critics often drew comparisons with the humanity and basic kindness at the heart of charity and argued that losing these was too high a price to pay for 'efficiency' or 'rationality'. The Irish-American poet John Boyle O'Reilly mocked what he called 'the organised charity, scrimped and iced, in the name of a cautious statistical Christ',[26] while the writer Ambrose Bierce acknowledged that 'indubitably much is wasted and some mischief done by indiscriminate giving', but argued that 'there is something to be said for "undirected relief" all the same' because 'it blesses not only him who receives, but him who gives'.[27] The American social reformer Jane Addams, herself a noted philanthropist, likewise wrote that

> even those of us who feel most sorely the need of more order in altruistic effort and see the end to be desired, find something distasteful in the juxtaposition of the words 'organised' and 'charity'. At bottom we distrust a scheme which substitutes a theory of social conduct for the natural promptings of the heart, even although we appreciate the complexity of the situation.[28]

The concerns of these critics were borne out in the early twentieth century, as prominent adherents of scientific philanthropy began to embrace eugenics and other deeply problematic doctrines as part of their efforts to rationalize giving. There had long been a link between questions of population and notions of charity, stretching back to the work of population theorist Thomas Malthus at the turn of the nineteenth century. His later admirers, such as the *Economist* editor Walter Bagehot, argued that

> great good, no doubt, philanthropy does, but then it also does great evil. It augments so much vice, it multiplies so much suffering, it brings to life such great populations to suffer and to be vicious, that it is open to argument whether it be or be not an evil to the world.[29]

The mid-nineteenth century saw the publication of Charles Darwin's *Origin of Species* (1859), expounding his initially controversial but hugely influential theory of evolution by natural selection, a theory that gained currency in its shorthand form of 'survival of the fittest'. Many subsequently tried to adapt Darwin's ideas to human society, as he himself attempted in his later book *The Descent of Man* (1871), where he argued that efforts to prevent the 'weak of body or mind' from marrying would be desirable in order to avoid 'the undoubtedly bad effects of the weak surviving and propagating their kind'.[30] Combined with better understanding of the mechanisms of genetic heredity, this 'social Darwinism' provided those concerned about population issues with the basis for ever-more active interventions, including compulsory birth control and forced sterilization.

Such ideas shock us now, but they were widely accepted across society, to the extent that by the 1920s hundreds of universities were offering courses on eugenics. Perhaps unsurprisingly, these ideas were particularly enthusiastically adopted by many proponents of scientific philanthropy, who saw them as powerful new tools in their efforts to improve society. Women's rights and birth control activists such as Marie Stopes and Margaret Sanger were also prominent promoters of eugenics. Likewise, a number of big-name US philanthropic foundations were involved in supporting eugenics research or the use of eugenic methods. The original funding for the Eugenics Research Office in the US, for instance, came from the Carnegie Corporation in 1910, while other foundations such as Ford, Rockefeller and Russell Sage supported similar efforts elsewhere.[31] The Chicago-based Wieboldt Foundation, meanwhile, funded a book on 'intelligent philanthropy' in 1930 that included contributions from a range of academic experts, including notorious eugenicist H.S. Jennings. In his chapter on 'biological aspects of charity', Jennings suggested that

> charitable organizations are promoting the survival and propagation of the unfit ... they are progressively filling the race with the weak and degenerate, who must hand on their weakness and degeneracy to their descendants. Conditions should be made harder instead of easier; any other procedure results in corrupting the race.[32]

Coming at a time when the Nazi Party was formulating its ideology in Germany – which would lead eventually to the atrocities and genocide of the Holocaust – these words in a book on philanthropy are especially chilling. Yet much later in the twentieth century, there were still instances of philanthropic organizations being involved with highly problematic population theories and practice; in the late 1970s, for instance, the Ford Foundation was involved in a funding programme aimed at addressing overpopulation in India that is now acknowledged to have coerced many men to be sterilized against their will.[33]

As we have seen, philanthropists long proclaimed the superiority of their approaches over more traditional charity precisely because they were rational and focused on 'causes not symptoms'. However, this can cut both ways. The ignominious legacy of philanthropy's entanglement with eugenics is one that we are still facing up to today and it acts as a stark reminder of what can happen if we lose sight of basic principles of empathy and human decency in the quest for clear-cut solutions to complex social problems. Perhaps, then, we should see philanthropy and charity less as a matter of either/or and more as both/and: the ideal being to balance the immediacy and human connection of charity with the rationality and universality of philanthropy? This, indeed, is what the feminist and social reformer Josephine Butler argued back in 1869, framing it in terms of what she saw as 'masculine' and 'feminine' approaches to philanthropy:

> We have had experience of what we may call the feminine form of philanthropy, and independent individual ministering, of too mediaeval a type to suit the present

> day. It has failed. We are now about to try the masculine form of philanthropy – large and comprehensive measures, organizations and systems planned by men and sanctioned by Parliament. This will also fail if it so far prevail as to extinguish the truth to which the other method witnessed in spite of its excess. Why should we not try at last a union of principles which are equally true?[34]

Butler's words were not heeded at the time, and in some senses philanthropy has continued to favour ever more the head over the heart. Many big donors still demonstrate a preference for technocratic, top-down approaches that put great distance between them and the people they support. This can lead to problems: Facebook founder Mark Zuckerberg's first major foray into philanthropy, for example, was an attempt to 'disrupt' the New Jersey public school system through the promotion of charter schools, which ran into furious opposition from teachers and parents who had not been consulted and resented having such 'philanthropic paternalism' imposed on them.

Recent years have also seen the rise of a powerful new force for promoting rationality in philanthropy in the shape of 'effective altruism'. This is a movement based on the utilitarian ethics of philosopher Peter Singer, which urges its followers to adopt a cause-neutral approach to giving in which the only aim is to maximize the amount of good your donation does (in terms of an appropriate objective measurement such as Quality Adjusted Life Years (QALYS)).[35] Like many previous efforts to impose greater rationality on philanthropy, effective altruism has attracted its fair share of criticism, but it has also gained many supporters, particularly among a new breed of donor who have made their fortune in the technology industry and are ideologically disposed towards approaches that are data-driven and rational.

Yet in other areas there are signs that the pendulum might be swinging back towards charity, with more emphasis on human connection and small-scale acts of kindness. A growing number of elite philanthropists are using their wealth to support work aimed at encouraging everyday giving: the Bill and Melinda Gates Foundation, for example, is a major supporter of the global generosity movement Giving Tuesday, which seeks to promote giving in its broadest sense through an annual day of giving (as well as other work throughout the year).

Other philanthropists are incorporating elements more traditionally associated with charity into their own giving, most notably Mackenzie Scott, the billionaire former wife of Amazon boss Jeff Bezos, who since 2019 has given away a remarkable $8.6 billion and counting. Scott's philanthropy is notable not only for its scale and pace, but also for her approach. By doing away with the top-down, programmatic approach that has been the norm in big money philanthropy since Carnegie and Rockefeller's day and instead focusing on giving unsolicited, no-strings-attached gifts to a wide array of nonprofits and grassroots organizations, she is challenging deeply ingrained received wisdom about how to give well. In doing so, Scott has repeatedly emphasized the importance of human connection and emotion. In one blog post she describes telephoning leaders of nonprofit organizations to inform them of a gift they are about to receive and being met with 'personal stories and tears', which 'invariably made me and my teammates cry'.

It is not yet clear whether Scott's emphasis on human connection is feasible at scale, or whether her approach will influence others and herald a shift towards new norms in philanthropy that put human connection back at its core. However, it was notable that in early 2022, following her divorce from husband Bill Gates, Melinda French Gates announced her intention to move the focus of her philanthropy away from the foundation she had for many years jointly run with him and instead focus on a new approach that prioritizes empowering those closest to the problems, and clearly echoes that adopted by Mackenzie Scott. Given the scale of the philanthropic resources that these two women have between them, they have the power to exert huge influence over how philanthropy is done, so perhaps this does mark an important turning point.

The rise of digital platforms as a key tool for giving is also having an impact on distinctions between philanthropy and charity. When people give via platforms and apps, it may be to traditional charitable organizations or nonprofits, but it is just as likely that they are donating in response to fundraising requests from individuals. Hence technology is bringing us back round to old models of giving based on peer-to-peer interaction and unmediated individual choice (without the limitations of geographical proximity of the past).

On the plus side, this could lead to more people giving, since being asked directly by an identifiable person is one of the things most likely to convince someone to donate. On the flip side, however, we might rediscover old challenges as people grapple with whether to treat their platform donations as charity or philanthropy. When people are faced with multiple requests to give, they may find themselves in the same position as those donors of the past who were overwhelmed by the volume of charitable entreaties, and as a result invented the voluntary association. Will the platform donors of today simply end up having to create mechanisms that replicate the function of traditional charitable organizations and thus reinvent the philanthropic wheel? Likewise, to choose between causes, we may well reintroduce problematic distinctions between 'deserving' and 'undeserving' recipients. And if those judgments are made without the involvement of intermediaries able to ensure that money goes to those in greatest need (as charities have done for so long), the situation is likely to be even worse, because the decisions will be subject to a whole range of biases, both conscious and unconscious. (There is already evidence, for instance, that when people give to crowdfunding campaigns for medical treatment, they are more likely to favour those of a similar racial profile to themselves or those who are most adept at utilizing social media to tell their story, rather than those in greatest need.)[36] Technology, then, may bring us full circle, back to very old models of giving, with all their challenges as well as their benefits.

3
PHILANTHROPY
OR JUSTICE?

'A society could make no greater mistake', wrote the US clergyman and president of Dartmouth College William Jewett Tucker in 1891, 'than asking charity to do the work of social justice.'[1] Many have shared this view: in 1932 the British Labour Party leader George Lansbury declared that his party could 'not accept charity as a substitute for social justice',[2] while in the same year philosopher Bertrand Russell argued that 'in a just world there would be no room for "charity"'.[3] Why has this distinction been seen as so important? And what can it tell us about the nature and role of philanthropy today?

We have already seen that philanthropy is tricky to define. Justice is, if anything, even harder; but let us settle for now on the *Oxford Dictionary of Philosophy* definition of it as something that 'in one sense is identical with the ethics of who should receive benefits and burdens, good or bad things of many sorts, given that others might also receive these things'. Is philanthropy – as a means of redistributing assets – a form of justice? And if philanthropy is not *inherently* just, can it be made to serve the demands of justice in some cases? Or, since inequality is arguably a precondition of philanthropy (as it requires there to be haves and have-nots), does philanthropy always reflect, or even prolong, existing injustice? Could philanthropy be *actively opposed* to justice?

The problem of tainted wealth

There have certainly been plenty of critics throughout history who have argued that philanthropy perpetuates injustice rather than addressing it. Sometimes these arguments are specific to certain models of philanthropy and in other cases they target philanthropy as a whole. An example of the first type is the longstanding claim that some donations are 'tainted' because they come from morally dubious sources. If the injustice perpetrated in making a fortune in the first place is sufficiently great, it is argued, then this outweighs any efforts to do good by giving it away, so that act of philanthropy cannot be just. The ethical dilemmas posed by tainted donations give rise to many challenging questions. What, for instance, qualifies a donor as tainted? Does that taint apply only to the donor or is it somehow transmitted via their money? How long does the taint last? And is it better for a recipient to accept the gift in the hope of putting 'bad money' to good uses or turn it down in order to avoid tainting oneself?

These are questions that people have been grappling with for as long as they have been giving to good causes and opinion has always been divided. Some have concluded that tainted money can never legitimately be put to good use through philanthropy; as far back as 746, for instance, the Council of Clovesho, a church synod attended by Anglo-Saxon kings, decreed that 'alms should not be given from goods unjustly plundered or otherwise extracted through force or cruelty'.[4] Likewise, in the nineteenth century the Quaker philanthropist George Cadbury took a holistic view that 'no amount of philanthropic giving could take the curse of a fortune that had been accumulated carelessly or without regard for the welfare of the workpeople who had laboured for it.'[5] And during his time in Britain in the 1840s, the American abolitionist and writer Frederick Douglass made his feelings about tainted donations quite clear by orchestrating a public campaign against the Free Church of Scotland's solicitation of gifts from American slave-owners, calling on the church to 'send the bloodstained money back'.[6]

Others, though, have argued that distinguishing between 'good' and 'bad' money is unworkable and should therefore not be an impediment to philanthropy. According to George Bernard Shaw,

> practically all the spare money in the country consists of
> a mass of rent, interest and profit, every penny of which
> is bound up with crime, drink, prostitution, disease and all

the evil fruits of poverty as inextricably as with enterprise, wealth, commercial probity and national prosperity. The notion that you can earmark certain coins as tainted is an unpractical individualist superstition.[7]

And Salvation Army founder 'General' William Booth (perhaps apocryphally) expressed it most clearly when he reportedly said that 'the only problem with tainted wealth is 't'aint enough of it!'

Figure 3.1: 'Puck's Inventions'. Cartoon by Samuel Ehrhart for *Puck* magazine, 12 April 1905

John D. Rockefeller stands on a ladder, dumping coins into a 'Patent Disinfector' as a member of the clergy opens a slot and coins pour into a bucket labelled 'Purified Cash for Missions'. This cartoon reflects the controversy over Rockefeller's donation to the American Board for Foreign Missions, which brought the arguments over 'tainted donations' to the mainstream of public and political debate in the early twentieth century.

Tainted donations became a major source of mainstream political debate in the early twentieth-century US, thanks primarily to a 1905 controversy over a large donation from John D. Rockefeller to the American Board of Commissioners for Foreign Missions. The American Board itself was bullish, arguing that acceptance of the gift did not equate to condoning Rockefeller's monopolistic approach to business, and that in any case their responsibility was to do good with the money rather than take a stance on the activities that generated it. Public and political opinion was not necessarily on their side, however; US President Theodore Roosevelt argued in a 1906 speech that 'we should discriminate in the sharpest way between fortunes well won and fortunes ill won', and that when it came to the latter, 'no amount of charity in spending such fortunes in any way compensated for misconduct in making them.'[8] A number of high profile satirists couldn't resist getting in on the act either. Mark Twain wrote a mocking letter to *Harper's Weekly* in the guise of Satan, which began: 'Dear Sir and Kinsman – Let us have done with this frivolous talk. The American Board accepts contributions from me every year: then why shouldn't it from Mr. Rockefeller ...?'[9] Fellow novelist G.K. Chesterton, meanwhile, penned an article entitled 'Gifts of the Millionaire' in which he poured scorn on Rockefeller's philanthropy, arguing that it was nothing more than the latest in a long line of tawdry attempts to buy absolution through giving and that as a result philanthropy was 'rapidly becoming the recognisable mark of a wicked man'.[10]

The spectre of tainted donations continues to loom large over modern philanthropy. In part this is due to concerns about wealth accrued long ago through profits from slavery or colonialism. In recent years a growing number of institutions have been forced to acknowledge the problematic nature of some of their past donors (and their present wealth) due to pressure from funders, campaigners and the public. This was amplified following the wave of Black Lives Matter protests around the world in 2020 sparked by the murder of George Floyd. At this point there were signs that an even more widespread historical reckoning might take place, as many organizations began to face up to their own pasts. Whether this results in genuine longer-term change in terms of how we deal with historically tainted wealth remains to be seen.

There are still complex and difficult debates ongoing about the appropriate response for funders and recipients when it comes to problematic historical links: is there any statute of limitation, for example, so the taint attached to a sum of money can be said to have expired after a certain period? Likewise, if money is still seen to be tainted, is it enough simply to acknowledge this? If a tainted donor is commemorated via a statue or their name on a building, does this need to be removed? Or is that merely tokenism, when in fact what is required is tangible reparation? To complicate matters further, this area has become highly politicized, tangled up in 'culture war' narratives, so that any decision is interpreted through ideological lenses. Removing the statue of a historical donor or taking their name off a building is seen by some as a 'woke rewriting of history', while doing nothing is taken by others as evidence of support for everything that individual stood for. Unfortunately, in this febrile atmosphere the nuance and complexity necessary for genuine understanding of the past tend to be among the first casualties; discussion of historically tainted donations often collapses into easy binaries or simplistic generalizations that don't get us closer to a proper understanding of how to navigate the challenges. In practical terms, a good first step is for organizations to commission research into the historical sources of their assets, so that we can at least reach well-informed judgments (even if we do not always draw the same conclusions).

Figure 3.2: 'The Effigies of the late Charitable Edward Colston, Esq.' Pamphlet sold in Bristol by Benjamin Rome after 1721

This eighteenth-century pamphlet was published shortly after the death of slave-owner, MP and philanthropist Edward Colston to highlight his extensive charitable work. Long a controversial figure in his home city of Bristol due to his close ties to the slave trade, Colston became the focus of a debate about our understanding and commemoration of problematic donors from the past after his statue was torn down and thrown into Bristol harbour by Black Lives Matter protesters in 2020.

Concerns about tainted donations are not restricted to dubious gifts from the past, of course. There are plenty of living donors whose giving poses ethical issues. Most notable in this regard in recent years has been the Sackler family, whose role in creating and profiting from the US opioid epidemic – as detailed in Patrick Radden Keefe's *Empire of Pain* – has led many cultural and higher education institutions that have benefitted from the Sacklers' money to declare that they will no longer accept their donations. In some cases, this includes removing the family's name from buildings. And the Sacklers are far from being the only example; in fact, if anything, tainted donation scandals are occurring with greater frequency than ever. Perhaps this is because greater scrutiny is enabling us to place philanthropic giving in a wider context so ethical concerns come to light more easily. Perhaps also the ethical criteria we apply have become more demanding, so a greater number of cases are now seen as problematic.

Whatever the reason, the issues raised by tainted wealth continue to pose real challenges for philanthropy. Donors may be increasingly wary of giving (or at least of doing so openly and transparently) if they feel this will put them in the firing line over how they made their money. Equally, cash-strapped organizations faced with ethically questionable donations need to decide whether they can justify taking the money or should refuse it, which involves grappling with complex issues. Does accepting the gift imply condoning the donor and thus risk making the recipient organization complicit

3.1 Thought experiment: Tainted donations

You're a university vice-chancellor. You're good at attracting talented people but securing the funding that could enable them to maximize their potential is a perennial problem. The founder of a technology business, which has recently been criticized for selling surveillance products to repressive regimes around the world, has just offered to make a major donation to fund a new Centre for Global Sustainability in their name. You need to brief your ethics committee, which will produce a report on whether you should accept the donation. What do you want them to take into account?

in reputation laundering? How does an organization balance the potential long-term reputational damage of accepting a questionable gift against the definite short-term financial damage of turning it down? Does the gift come with strings attached, so that the donor is able to exert control over how it is spent, or is it entirely at arm's length? In practical terms, many organizations are now trying to establish consistent donation acceptance policies that can provide a framework to answer such questions (even if the actual decisions often have to be made case by case).

If a gift has already been accepted, things are even more complicated because it is not always legally possible to return it. Likewise, new technological developments bring further challenges; there is a growing trend towards 'crypto-philanthropy', for instance, in which

Figure 3.3: The front entrance of the Serpentine Gallery in London in 2014, bearing the Sackler name

The Sackler family were for a long time best known as generous philanthropists and patrons of the arts. Yet as awareness grew of the role that their family-owned company, Purdue Pharma, played in creating and perpetuating the US opioid crisis, a growing number of organizations and institutions that had previously accepted the Sackler's gifts became concerned about ethical issues around 'tainted donations'. Like many others, the Serpentine Gallery removed the Sackler name in 2021, though they maintained their decision was not linked to concerns about the family's reputation.

people make donations in cryptocurrencies such as Bitcoin or Ethereum. Since these cryptocurrencies are designed to maintain the privacy of users, charities that accept crypto donations find themselves faced with real challenges when it comes to ascertaining the source of their funds, because they are unable to do the required due diligence. Children International and the Water Project found themselves in this situation in 2020, when it transpired that a $10,000 donation made via a crypto giving platform had come from money stolen by the hacker group Darkside.[11] Tainted donations, therefore, look set to be just as much, if not more, of an issue in the future.

'It is justice, not charity, that is wanting in the world'

The notion of tainted donations reflects a concern over money made in ways which create injustice that cannot be undone by giving it away. There is, however, a more fundamental criticism which argues that *all* philanthropy is in tension with justice because it stems from unequal and unjust systems, while doing nothing to challenge them (and in fact, some have argued, actively impedes wider efforts to seek justice). This argument emerged during the Enlightenment (although its roots go back much further), when traditional religious notions of poverty as something that reflected a natural order imposed by God were replaced by a new secular view of poverty as a structural failing in society. This meant that, for the first time, poverty was seen as something that could potentially be fixed, rather than something to be accepted. Consequently justice no longer entailed simply ensuring that the existing rules of society were enforced; it require abandoning those rules for new ones.

To understand why these changes took place, we need to take a brief look at how people have thought about the nature of property (since charity and philanthropy are in large part about the transfer of property between the 'haves' and the 'have-nots' in a society so, as the philosopher J.B. Schneewind argues, 'a serious history of thought about charity would be inseparable from a history of thought about property').[12] For medieval Christians, property was put on Earth by God in such a way that some people would be rich and others poor. The rich were not seen as owners of their property, but merely stewards during their lifetimes, with a duty to give back to the poor (up to a point) through almsgiving. As Thomas Aquinas put it in his *Summa Theologica* (1485), 'man ought to possess external things, not as his own, but as common; so that, to wit, he is ready to communicate them to others in their need'.[13] Furthermore, it was seen as a *good* thing that there were poor people, both because they were closer to God (hence the famous teaching that it was easier for a camel to pass through the eye of a needle than for a rich man to enter heaven) and because the

Figure 3.4: 'Works of mercy: just as water extinguishes fire, so works of mercy (with penitence) extinguish sin.' Engraving attributed to T. Galle, 1601

The foreground of this engraving depicts a group of almoners (church officials tasked with distributing money to the deserving poor). In the background is Noah's Ark, surrounded by floodwaters and drowning people. The picture asks us to compare how charitable giving washes away sins with the Biblical flood sent by God washing away humanity's sins.

existence of the poor gave the rich an opportunity to prove their worth through charity.

The Enlightenment brought radical new ideas about the nature of property, marking a shift away from the medieval idea that property reflected a natural order imposed by God, but there were markedly different schools of thought about what this meant. One school of thought – rooted in the work of Hugo Grotius and Samuel von Pufendorf in the seventeenth century – argued that while justifying property ownership should no longer rely on appeal to a deity, nor was property simply a product of human institutions: it reflected 'natural law' and 'natural property rights', which were prior to any human-designed laws or rights.[14] The most famous version of this view was set out by the seventeenth-century English philosopher John Locke, who argued that property rights were grounded in an individual's right to claim ownership over that part of the world that they had carved out of the state of nature by their own labour.[15] And this set the stage for the key question that shaped thinking about charity and justice for the next hundred years and more: is giving a choice or a duty?

Some proponents of natural rights, such as Grotius, maintained that charity was entirely a matter of choice: since people could now be considered owners of their property (rather than merely stewards) there was nothing compelling them to give, though they were obviously free to do so if they wished. Others, such as Pufendorf and Locke, argued that the right to property was still accompanied by a duty to give charitably out of any excess, even if the nature of this duty was hazy. This required them to draw a crucial distinction between two kinds of duty: *perfect* duties are those that carry with them a clear specification of what is demanded of the subject, who the recipient is and the nature of the recipient's rights in respect of the duty. *Imperfect* duties, on the other hand, require the subject to do something, but do not specify exactly what or for whom. Duties of charity, it was argued, are imperfect duties, and this distinguishes them from duties of justice, which are perfect.

This distinction was also important to the other school of thought on the nature of property that emerged during the Enlightenment, which agreed with Locke et al. that the distribution of property was not ordained by God, but disagreed with their idea that it was based on an alternative conception of natural rights that would still ensure justice. In fact, it was argued, the unequal distribution of wealth is unjust, a reflection of flawed societal structures which can only be remedied through radical reform. An early proponent of this view in the seventeenth century was the English religious reformer and political radical Gerrard Winstanley, whose True Levellers (or 'Diggers') were a group of protestors who sought to reclaim formerly common land that had been privatized by enclosure. They believed that there was more than enough land for everyone in society but that unjust and unnatural notions of property had prevented it being shared fairly.[16]

For those like Winstanley who believed that poverty and inequality were man-made, the claims of the poor to a greater share of society's riches were not requests for charity but demands for justice. Furthermore, charity – as an imperfect duty and a matter of free choice – could not by itself achieve justice. In fact, the presence of charity may even get in the way of justice being done, by alleviating the symptoms of poverty and so undermining the momentum for radical change. This point of view came to fruition in the late eighteenth century and is reflected in the writings of many prominent thinkers, such as pioneering women's rights advocate Mary Wollstonecraft, who declared that 'it is justice, not charity, that is wanting in the world' and argued that to the rich 'the rights of men are grating sounds that set their teeth on edge' so that 'if the poor are in distress, they will make some *benevolent* exertions to assist them; they will confer obligations, but not do justice.'[17] Her husband, the political philosopher William Godwin, agreed, decrying what he saw as 'a system of clemency and charity, instead of a system of justice', which resulted in the poor being forced into a position of servility in which they 'regard the slender comforts they obtain, not as their incontrovertible due, but as the good pleasure and grace of their opulent neighbours.'[18] Thomas Paine, the political radical whose writing heavily influenced the American revolution, was likewise clear that 'it is not charity but a right, not bounty but justice' he was seeking, and that for him 'the present state of civilization is as odious as it is unjust', which meant that 'a revolution should be made in it.'[19] Even the German philosopher Immanuel Kant, not normally

seen as a radical, argued along similar lines in his
Lecture on Ethics:

> although we may be entirely within our rights, according
> to the laws of the land and the rules of our social structure,
> we may nevertheless be participating in a general injustice,
> and in giving to an unfortunate man we do not give him
> a gratuity but only help to return to him that of which the
> general injustice of our system has deprived him.[20]

The tension between charity and justice continued to
be a major source of debate for writers and thinkers
throughout the nineteenth and early twentieth
centuries. The French sociologist Émile Durkheim
wrote that 'no matter how obligatory it may be, charity
must never conflict with justice ... whenever a conflict
arises between these two kinds of duty, justice should
take precedence.'[21] Others suggested that charity and
justice were locked in a zero-sum game, in which the
success of one entailed the failure of the other; the
French novelist Émile Zola wrote of 'the new hope
– Justice, after eighteen hundred years of impotent
charity'.[22] Inevitably this became caught up in the
development of new thinking on the rights of the
working class and attacks on charity became a staple of
socialist polemic. Friedrich Engels, for instance, angrily
denounced philanthropic institutions for 'first sucking
out the very life-blood' of the proletariat and then
practising 'self-complacent, Pharisaic philanthropy
upon them', which 'gives back to the plundered
victims the hundredth part of what belongs to them'.[23]

Oscar Wilde likewise claimed that the poor felt charity to be 'a ridiculously inadequate mode of partial restitution' and asked, 'why should they be grateful for the crumbs that fall from the rich man's table?' Rather, he argued 'they should be seated at the board, and are beginning to know it.'[24]

The charity/justice distinction became even more important in the twentieth century as a diverse range of new social movements fought for new rights for previously marginalized communities. Many individuals and organizations within these movements benefitted from philanthropic support, but this was not enough and could even be harmful, supporters argued, if it was always framed as a matter of discretionary benevolence rather than of justice and rights. The civil rights leader Dr Martin Luther King acknowledged this problem in 1963 when he famously said that 'philanthropy is commendable, but it must not cause us to overlook the circumstances of economic injustice which make philanthropy necessary.'[25] Others were more vociferous in their condemnation of what they saw as philanthropy's tendency to prop up existing systems and structures and thereby to get in the way of reform that could deliver justice. The writer Langston Hughes decried

the lovely grinning face of Philanthropy – which gives a million dollars to a Jim Crow school, but not one job to a graduate of that school; which builds a Negro hospital with second-rate equipment, then commands black patients and student doctors to go there whether they will or no.[26]

The leaders of the Zapatista indigenous rights movement in Mexico declared that 'pity is an affront, and charity is a slap in the face'.[27] This sentiment was shared by many in the disability rights movement, who felt the distinction between charity and justice particularly keenly since disabled people had traditionally been seen as objects of pity (and therefore the archetypal recipients of charity). From the mid-twentieth century, however, new voices emerged within the disabled community urging disabled people to reject charity and instead to demand equal rights and representation as citizens, under slogans such as 'justice, not charity' and 'nothing about us without us'.

From generosity to justice?

The debate over charity's relationship to justice continues to shape views on what philanthropy is for and how it should be done today. There are those who argue, like Wollstonecraft and Paine, that philanthropy is an inadequate means of achieving justice and that we should instead focus on restructuring society more fundamentally to address inequality. The prominent philanthropy critic Anand Giridharadas brought this argument to a mainstream audience with his 2018 bestseller *Winners Take All*, in which he insisted that 'generosity is not a substitute for justice'. For Giridharadas and others who share his view, the proposed solution is usually taxing wealth more effectively, as this would serve justice better by boosting the state's resources. (This then introduces a tension between philanthropy and taxation, as we shall see in Chapter 4.)

Others accept that while justice is important, abandoning philanthropy entirely is neither feasible nor desirable. Rather, they argue, we must ask how the demands of justice require us to do philanthropy differently. At one end of the spectrum, this can lead to radical new interpretations of the purpose of giving; the political philosopher Chiara Cordelli, for example, argues that 'philanthropy should be understood foremost as a duty of reparative justice'.[28] In her view there is a moral compulsion on individuals (particularly wealthy ones) to give, but when they do, they should act as if they have no personal discretion over where their donations go – instead those donations should be directed at addressing the injustice and inequality that allowed the wealth creation in the first place. For most who believe that philanthropy has a role to play in our society and have experience of how it works, rejecting donor freedom to this extent is probably a step too far. Instead, attention has focused on a both/and approach: balancing individual choice regarding giving with the desire to make the whole system more equitable and just. This is neatly exemplified by Ford Foundation president Darren Walker, who invoked the legacy of both Martin Luther King and Andrew Carnegie in the title of his 2020 book *From Generosity to Justice: A New Gospel of Wealth*. Walker has repeatedly argued for the need for a new approach to philanthropy that makes justice its core aim.

How then, in practical terms, can philanthropy better serve the needs of justice? For a start, we need to address the concerns about tainted wealth we explored earlier in this chapter. At an individual level, this means grappling with the ethical issues that come from accepting donations and from offering recognition to donors who have made their money in ways that cause harm. At systemic level, it means facing up to the problematic histories of our systems of wealth generation and the injustices they have caused, as well as to sources of wealth that still pose problems today. The author and activist Edgar Villanueva has proposed we 'decolonize philanthropy' by acknowledging that many philanthropic assets come from systems with their roots in slavery, colonialism and White power, and then acting on this by adopting an appropriately reparative approach to giving.[29]

To ensure that philanthropy furthers justice, we also need to frame it with respect to tax. No philanthropy can be just if the donor has not already paid the tax that they owe. To put it in the terms we used earlier: we must first meet our *perfect* duties to society by paying taxes, then meet our *imperfect* duties through giving (and we might even freely give more than is demanded by any duty – the fancy word for which is 'supererogatory' giving). Simply paying existing taxes may not be enough, however, if those taxes fail to match the scale of inequality – in which case there is an additional onus on justice-minded philanthropists to support calls for higher taxes too. This is precisely what groups like Patriotic Millionaires and Millionaires for

Humanity are doing: bringing together wealthy people, many of whom are already significant philanthropic donors, who believe that they and others like them need to pay far higher taxes in addition to their giving. A 2020 letter published by Millionaires for Humanity in response to the challenges of the COVID-19 pandemic and signed by eighty-three rich individuals from around the world, argued that

> The problems caused by, and revealed by, COVID-19 can't be solved with charity, no matter how generous. Government leaders must take the responsibility for raising the funds we need and spending them fairly. We can ensure we adequately fund our health systems, schools, and security through a permanent tax increase on the wealthiest people on the planet, people like us.[30]

Making philanthropy a tool for social justice is also about what we support and how we support it. Even if philanthropy is a matter of choices rather than rights, there is nothing to stop those choices being used to support organizations and social movements that are pushing for fundamental reform to existing systems and structures or demanding new rights for marginalized groups and communities. And this is a role that philanthropy has often (though far from always) fulfilled. The anti-slavery movement in Britain, for instance, relied heavily on philanthropy throughout the late eighteenth and early nineteenth centuries. Some of this support came from notable individuals such as the brewer Thomas Fowell Buxton or the statistician Zachary Macaulay (father of historian and politician Thomas Babington Macaulay), but there was also widespread support from everyday donors. Indeed, historian David Owen suggests that it was 'a movement supported chiefly, at least in its later stages, by large numbers of people in moderate or modest circumstances'.[31] Philanthropy likewise played a crucial role in the development of the women's movement in early twentieth-century America, with historian Joan Marie Johnson arguing that 'suffrage was only won when rich women gave large contributions'.[32]

Philanthropic support is often particularly vital in the early stages of a social movement's development, because funders can go against the status quo by supporting causes that are unpopular or have little public awareness. In doing so, they often bring mainstream legitimacy that is just as valuable as their financial resources. This 'philanthropic soft power' has played a crucial part in bringing many issues from the margins to the mainstream and ensuring that social movements have been able to secure changes to laws, policies and public opinion that have made our society fairer and more equal.

We should be careful not to overstate the case here. While there are plenty of great examples of philanthropy helping achieve key milestones of social progress – from the abolition of slavery to the decriminalization of homosexuality – funding for social justice remains a relatively small part of the overall landscape. And even when philanthropy has seemingly focused on justice by supporting social movements, this has not always been plain sailing. Many critics have noted the risk that when large, resource-rich funders encounter small, resource-poor social movements, the funder will skew the focus of the movement or soften its edges (even if this is unintended). The political scientist Megan Ming Francis has explored the interaction in the early twentieth century between the American Fund for Public Service (often known as the Garland Fund, and one of the most progressive foundations of the era) and the National Association for the Advancement of Colored People (NAACP). She identifies a process of 'movement capture' in which the Garland fund 'used their financial leverage to redirect the NAACP's agenda away from the issue of racial violence to a focus on education at a critical juncture in the civil rights movement.'[33] Other scholars such as Karen Ferguson and Alice O'Connor have noted similar issues arising with the Ford Foundation's funding of parts of the civil rights movement in the 1960s.[34]

The interaction between philanthropic funders and social movements is thus fraught with challenges that must be navigated if philanthropy is genuinely to advance social justice. An important part of doing this is recognizing the need to shift power, as well as financial resources, to the organizations receiving support and to the communities directly affected. Our traditional models of philanthropy, many of them rooted in the paternalistic approaches of the nineteenth and early twentieth centuries, are not necessarily well suited to this. These models need to change. One possibility is to move away from restricted, programmatic funding

– which leaves the power to determine how money is used in the hands of the donor – and instead adopt a trust-based approach, in which funding is provided to recipient organizations with no strings attached, in the belief that they know best how to spend money to achieve their aims. More radically, an increasing number of philanthropic funders are experimenting with participatory methods of grantmaking, in which those who would traditionally have been seen as the passive beneficiaries of philanthropic gifts become active participants in decision-making about resource allocation. This is not an entirely new idea; the Haymarket People's Fund in Boston, Massachusetts, for instance, has been using participatory methods since its founding in 1974. However, they remain very much in a minority, and while there has certainly been more talk about participatory grantmaking in recent years, there is also a clear gap between rhetoric and reality. We should be wary of seeing this kind of approach as a panacea in any case, but it has the potential to be an important part of shifting the balance within philanthropy from charity to justice.

4
PHILANTHROPY OR THE STATE?

'It seems to me', wrote Anton Chekhov in 1891, 'that one will do nothing by means of philanthropy ... To make something of great importance dependent on charity is pernicious. I should prefer it to be financed out of the Government treasury.'[1] This highlights one of the most important questions when it comes to determining what philanthropy is for: what should we expect the state to do in terms of meeting the welfare needs of citizens, and what is it acceptable (or even desirable) to leave to voluntary efforts? This is a question that has received wildly different answers over the years, which reflect divergent views about the nature of society and fundamental dividing lines between political ideologies. To understand these different views and how they still shape our thinking, we need to look back at how the relationship between philanthropy and the state developed: it's a relationship that has often been collaborative, and sometimes combative, but never straightforward.

The state and philanthropy – rivals or partners?

Philanthropy and state provision are sometimes presented by those on both sides of the political spectrum as if they are locked in a zero-sum game, where any increase in one must mean a decrease in the other. Small-state advocates argue that government crowds out voluntary activity and that if taxation and public spending were cut back we would see an upsurge in philanthropy. Those favouring a larger role for the state, conversely, argue that philanthropic provision is inadequate in both scale and distribution, and that the only way to address this failing is for the government to tax and spend more. Both views contain a kernel of truth, but neither is entirely right: philanthropy and state welfare have co-existed for hundreds of years in a complex balance in which each shapes and is shaped by the other.

Questions of state responsibility for welfare (in the UK at least) only begin to make sense in around the sixteenth century. Prior to this, according to one of the first historians of English philanthropy Benjamin Kirkman Gray, the state essentially saw its role as 'the maintenance of power by means of the maximum of revenue' and 'had not yet accepted as its task the furthering of the welfare of the whole body of citizens.'[2] Welfare was primarily the responsibility of the family or the church, either informally or through local institutions such as almshouses, monasteries and hospitals. The Reformation, with its seizure of monastic assets, decimated this existing welfare infrastructure and, by the end of the sixteenth century, the loss of these systems of support contributed to poverty becoming so severe that the government was forced to introduce the Poor Laws of 1598 and 1601. Tension between state provision and philanthropy was baked into the model from the outset. The 1601 Poor Laws were accompanied by the Statute of Charitable Uses, a piece of legislation ostensibly designed to address concerns about the accountability of charitable trusts but in reality, according to historian James Fishman, a key tool in the Tudor government's efforts to 'use charitable contributions to relieve poverty and thereby make unnecessary the unpopular imposition of taxes at the parish level'.[3]

Over time, the state did (somewhat reluctantly) accept a great share of responsibility for meeting welfare needs. Crises such as epidemics, famine and wars often accelerated this process. As W.K. Jordan writes, 'these frightful visitations of epidemic taught the nation much regarding its own resources and disciplined it in the understanding that the poverty bred by plague must be instantly relieved lest even more terrible social consequences should ensue.'[4] More broadly, the backdrop of growing urbanization and industrialization significantly altered the scale and nature of poverty and the challenges facing the populace. This was a big factor in pushing the state towards meeting welfare needs, especially after the introduction of the census in 1801 since, according to Benjamin Kirkman Gray, 'once the state had assumed the responsibility of knowing how the people lived it could not ignore the general misery of their condition.'[5] We also saw in Chapter 2 that urbanization was a key factor in driving the development of new models of voluntary association from the eighteenth century, which led to the emergence of a meaningful public sphere in which citizens could undertake activities in an organized way that was not controlled by state or church. The proliferation of new civil society organizations meant that even as the state assumed more responsibility for welfare, it still took a very deliberate back seat to philanthropic provision; according to the 1952 Nathan Committee report, 'the state filled in gaps in charity rather than charity filling in gaps left by the state.'[6] Even as the state moved into new areas, as historian Pat Thane has noted, it didn't necessarily do so directly; instead 'it first subsidised the existing pioneering work of voluntary organisations'.[7] And this was seen by many, particularly during the Victorian era, as the most desirable state of affairs. An editorial in *The Times* in 1856 sums up this attitude:

> Among the many considerations which make an Englishman proud of his country there is hardly one which can so justly excite his patriotic satisfaction as the contemplation of its vast, numerous and richly endowed charities. Much of that which the church or the state has collectively done in other countries, the voluntary benevolence of individuals has done in this ... it rarely,

very rarely happens that in England any great scheme
of comprehensive benevolence is initiated by the
Government, which is only too happy to await the results of
private enterprise and private experience.[8]

Then around the turn of the twentieth century, people
increasingly began to question whether the grand
Victorian project of trying to meet welfare needs
through charity should be abandoned, or at very least
augmented by significant increases in state involvement.
The Liberal governments of the early twentieth century
certainly believed so and brought in legislation such
as the 1911 National Insurance Act, which introduced
state pensions to address poverty in old age. Liberals
still valued voluntary action and were keen to ensure
it was not supplanted by state action. The same cannot
necessarily be said of all in the Labour movement, many
of whom were much more critical of philanthropy
and charity. The Labour intellectual Harold Laski
wrote in the 1940s that it was 'better to tackle social
problems without the intervention of gracious ladies
or benevolent busybodies or stockbrokers to whom
a hospital is a hobby'.[9] Views like these came into
the political mainstream following the election of the
post-war Labour government, through figures such as
Aneurin Bevan. Bevan's dislike of philanthropy, which
he derided as a 'patch-quilt of local paternalisms', was
evident in his declaration to the House of Commons
that 'it is repugnant to a civilised community for
hospitals to have to rely upon private charity.'[10] Many
of the key intellectual architects of the welfare state,

such as William Beveridge, had assumed an ongoing role for voluntary effort and philanthropy in all areas of welfare provision. Indeed, in the view of the 1952 Nathan Committee, it was 'clear that Parliament, so far from wishing to exclude voluntary effort, expected and intended that there should be a close partnership between the charitable organisations and the public authorities'.[11] Bevan, however, disagreed and ensured that in the final version of the National Health Service Act (1948) there was a far greater degree of centralization and state control than had been foreseen and voluntary organizations were largely excluded.

Not all in the Labour movement shared Bevan's dislike of voluntary action. Prime minister Clement Attlee, for one, was far more positive, arguing that 'this country will never become a people of an exclusive and omnipotent State' and that in his view 'we shall always have alongside the great range of public services, the voluntary services which humanise our national life and bring it down from the general to the particular.'[12] Over time, as gaps and failures in state provision became apparent, it was clear that obituaries for philanthropy by those who saw it as merely a precursor to a universal welfare state had been premature. Instead, philanthropy recast its role. In some cases, this meant working with the government (but now as a junior partner); in others it meant finding gaps in state provision and filling them; and in others still it meant putting energy into advocacy and campaigning work designed to challenge the welfare state's failings. This last role became ever more important as changes across society in the 1960s and 1970s led to a new spirit of activism and demand for participation, and the formation of campaigning organizations such as the housing and homelessness charity Shelter and the Child Poverty Action Group.

In the 1980s and 1990s, the emergence of public sector outsourcing gave rise to a further dimension in the relation between state and philanthropy. There was now renewed emphasis on the idea of voluntary organizations being involved in welfare provision, but instead of doing it separately from or alongside the state, they would do it on a contractual basis on *behalf* of the state. This meant that the balance of power in determining which needs were to be met, and how, shifted significantly away from the voluntary sector and into the hands of the state. It also put voluntary organizations in competition with commercial providers; decisions were often based on lowest cost rather than any wider measure of value, bringing the risk of a race to the bottom in terms of quality of provision.

The relationship between state and philanthropy in the UK has thus evolved in three distinct directions: there are areas in which charitable organizations continue to meet needs that the state does not take responsibility for (including surprising examples like hospices and lifeboats); there are areas in which charitable organizations have stood aside in favour of state provision (though they often still play a vital role in holding the state to account); and there are areas in which charitable organizations work with the state to meet welfare needs (increasingly in the role of contractual providers).

Philanthropy and state welfare today

The story just recounted is particular to the UK, and the history and current context in other countries may be markedly different. In places such as Cuba or Lao People's Democratic Republic a centralized state still controls many aspects of its citizens' lives, including meeting their welfare needs, with little room left for civil society or philanthropy. In other places, such as China, policies of social and economic liberalization have led to a growth in philanthropy that may be welcomed by the state but accompanied by a desire to control philanthropy and shape it in its own image. At the other end of the spectrum there are countries where philanthropy has been seen by many as preferable to state provision, most notably the US, where a strong streak of rugged individualism and suspicion of centralized government has long meant that philanthropy is looked to ahead of the state.

Despite differences between countries, however, one fundamental question remains relevant everywhere: what role should philanthropy play in relation to state provision of welfare? While there is clearly no single answer to this – as there will inevitably be deep divides in opinion depending on ideology, culture and history – it is possible to identify the main choices we need to make. First, is philanthropy seen as a direct alternative to state provision? This has clearly been the case at times throughout history, and during recent periods of economic hardship and austerity in which public finances have been strained, philanthropy has sometimes had to step into the breach. Perhaps the most extreme example was in the US city of Detroit in 2014, when as part of a 'Grand Bargain' struck to bail the city out of bankruptcy, a group of philanthropic foundations committed $816 million to prevent the sale of publicly owned artworks and protect the pensions of municipal workers.[13] In this context, it is undoubtedly tempting for cash-strapped public bodies to see philanthropy as a magic money tap that can alleviate pressure on government spending. Yet this would be a mistake.

The story of efforts to meet Britain's welfare needs primarily through philanthropy in the Victorian era was, in the end, one of failure. Benjamin Kirkman Gray, surveying the situation in 1905, wrote that 'private individuals were confident of their power to discharge a public function, and the government was willing to have it so. It was left to experience to determine that the work was ill done and was by no means equal to the need.'[14] Those who look to philanthropy as an alternative to public spending today are likely to be similarly disappointed, as the differences in both scale and distribution make it unsuited to this role. Even many of the world's biggest philanthropists acknowledge these limitations; Bill Gates has called philanthropy a 'rounding error' in comparison to public spending[15] and Michael Bloomberg (a man with experience in both philanthropy and public office) has said that 'all the billionaires added together are *bupkis* compared to the amount of money that government spends'.[16] Likewise the profile of where philanthropic money goes in no way matches up to that of public spending on society's needs. This is unsurprising given that philanthropy is still fundamentally about the individual choices of donors, which are shaped by a complex mixture of factors including upbringing, religious belief and life experience. This is in many ways a strength, as the core idea of a gift freely given has a power that should not be underestimated. But it also means that philanthropy is not good at providing consistency or equity at systemic level or ensuring an effective matching of supply to need – and these *are* features that we should want from public spending. Philanthropy is not a suitable replacement.

If philanthropy cannot be an alternative to state provision of welfare, what role *should* it play? We have already seen that in the history of the UK, philanthropy adapted to the creation of the welfare state by refocusing towards filling gaps in state provision while also challenging it through advocacy and campaigning, both of which remain important today. But philanthropy influences the state through showing, not just telling, as in addition to campaigning for reform, civil society organizations also model different way of meeting needs. In fact, this ability to foster innovation is often cited as one of philanthropy's key advantages over the state (a claim we shall look at further in the next chapter). This might mean finding better ways of delivering services that the state already provides, perhaps by making them more joined up and individually tailored, which voluntary organizations can do better because they are not confined to the same geographic and departmental siloes as the public sector. Or it might mean demonstrating the need for entirely new services and nudging the state to adapt in response to citizens' changing needs. As William Beveridge put it, while 'the democracy can and should learn to do what used to be done for public good by the wealthy', there always remains the challenge of 'getting the democracy to give for new things, and unfamiliar needs'.[17]

The other pertinent point we can take from the historical development of the philanthropy/state relationship in the UK is that crises such as wars and epidemics tend to lead to significant shifts in public attitudes about where the balance of responsibility for meeting welfare needs should lie. The limitations of voluntary provision laid bare by the many plague outbreaks of the sixteenth and seventeenth centuries, for instance, led to increasing centralization and state intervention; while the spirit of collectivism fostered by two world wars in the twentieth century paved the way for the eventual introduction of the welfare state (which, as we have seen, had a significant impact on the role of philanthropy). The COVID-19 pandemic which began in 2020 has once again brought many of the same questions to the fore. In the UK the public imagination was captured by the efforts of ninety-nine-year-old army veteran Captain Tom Moore, whose fundraising walk around his garden during the first period of lockdown raised over £30 million in donations. Yet at the same time many expressed unease at the idea that philanthropic donations were necessary to underpin the work of the National Health Service (NHS), which is often take as the paradigm of state-provided welfare. (In part this betrayed a general lack of awareness of the fact that many charities have long played a role within the NHS, providing the sort of gap-filling and added value that we outlined above, but it clearly struck a nerve.)

The COVID-19 pandemic raised similar questions elsewhere around the world about the relative responses of philanthropy and the state, and how we should look to meet society's future needs. For some, the pandemic highlighted the flexibility and speed of philanthropy, as funders and charitable organizations responded quickly to changing needs and played a variety of roles in response to the crisis (from frontline community services to the development of vaccines). For others, however, the lesson of the pandemic was that challenges of this scale and nature can only be dealt with through state action; since ongoing concerns about the unequal distribution of resources within countries and the failure to ensure the equitable distribution of vaccines around the world exposed once again the dangers of relying on philanthropy. Given that the impacts of climate breakdown and the fraying of many established social and geopolitical norms will lead to further crises around the world in years to come, these tensions will only get more pronounced. Hence it is vital that we face up to the question of where to draw the boundaries between state and philanthropy if we are to have any hope of understanding what philanthropy is for (even if this is not a question that can necessarily be given a permanent answer, since those boundaries will continue to shift over time).

Taxation

In order to spend money, governments need to raise it, which they do primarily through taxation. But if we believe that philanthropy has a role to play alongside the state in providing welfare, how should this be reflected in the tax system? Some argue that it should not be reflected at all: taxation and philanthropy should be kept entirely separate. It is fine to give, these critics would allow, but this is a matter of individual choice and we should only be free to give once we have met our duties by paying all the tax we owe. Philanthropy should certainly not be used to justify paying less tax, and it should not receive any special treatment from the state in the form of tax incentives either. This was the argument made by the UK Chancellor of the Exchequer Sir Robert Horne in 1922, when he proclaimed that

> charitable gifts should be made after a man has performed his ordinary obligations. The ordinary person's gifts to charity are those which he makes after paying his Income Tax. He pays Income Tax as a citizen of the country and what he gives in charity, he deprives himself of – that is the only charitable gift worth having, or at any rate the only one which should be commended.[18]

In practice, most countries around the world today not only allow philanthropy but actively encourage it through tax incentives. Why? Justifications fall broadly into three categories, as identified by the political philosopher Rob Reich.[19] The first is the 'tax base rationale', which argues that incentives for charitable giving are not really tax 'breaks' at all, as any charitable gifts need to be deducted from an individual's income to properly define what that person should be taxed on, since we should only be taxed on personal consumption or wealth accumulation, and money given away counts as neither. This appears to have been what Benjamin Disraeli was getting at when he claimed during a parliamentary debate on charity taxation in 1863 that 'exemption is not a privilege, but a right'[20] (although it is also possible that he was just trying to annoy his long-time political adversary William Gladstone, who took a different view and had just proposed measures to limit the tax privileges of charities). The problem with the tax base rationale is that it rests on the mere fact that money has been given away, without considering the *purpose* behind it. This means that there is no real basis on which to differentiate between charitable gifts and gifts that most people would not see as deserving of tax relief (such as gifts to a family member or political party). Some might argue that the altruistic or selfless nature of philanthropic donations makes them distinctive, but this is a difficult claim to back up: giving money away to charity is still a discretionary use of private wealth and cannot always be said to be entirely selfless

Figure 4.1: 'A Word to Grand Stand Specialists'. Cartoon by Samuel Ehrhart for *Puck* magazine, 3 June 1903

This cartoon shows Puck tugging at the coat-tails of Andrew Carnegie, as he and John D. Rockefeller pile money bags around the base of a statue labelled 'Fame', which they seek by endowing libraries and universities. Puck is suggesting that they could do more good by endowing places like a 'Home for Consumptives'. This image reflects the view that big-money philanthropy is often driven by a desire for reputation and social status.

as there are often clear benefits to donors from making gifts – whether concrete (having a museum wing named after them) or intangible (the warm glow of increased wellbeing and personal satisfaction).

The second broad justification for offering tax breaks on philanthropy is the 'subsidy rationale'. This is neatly captured by a 1939 report from the US House of Representatives, which declared that

the exemption from taxation of money or property devoted to charitable and other purposes is based upon the theory

that the Government is compensated for the loss of revenue
by its relief from financial burden which would otherwise
have to be met by appropriation from public funds.[21]

According to this logic, tax relief on philanthropic
donations is justified to the extent that the money
foregone in taxes results in the production of public
goods that the state would otherwise have to provide.
This brings us back to the arguments rehearsed
earlier as to why philanthropy should not be seen
as a viable replacement for public spending (because
neither the scale nor the distribution match up to the
requirements). Unfortunately, despite that clear reason
for rejecting this rationale, it still seems to be the case
that some form of the subsidy rationale is often in the
minds of policymakers and legislators (consciously or
not) when it comes to considering the question of tax
relief on philanthropy.

Since neither of the justifications considered so far
works, the final option is the 'pluralism rationale'.
This too argues that tax breaks for philanthropy
should be understood as subsidies, but not subsidies
for specific services or outcomes that the state would
otherwise have to provide; rather, they are *generalized*
subsidies for the maintenance of a healthy, pluralistic
civil society. Now it does not matter that the profile
of philanthropic giving does not match up with public
spending; in fact, that is arguably a good thing,
because if we are no longer viewing philanthropy as
a direct substitute for public spending then we should
surely want it to fund different things (even if there is

inevitably some overlap). A further benefit of adopting the pluralism rationale is that it provides a justification for extending tax reliefs to philanthropic support for things the government would never provide, such as campaigning and advocacy work to challenge government policy or push for fundamental structural reform. This makes sense, the argument goes, because the government acknowledges the inherent value of a vibrant civil society, including its role in holding those in power to account. Of course, it is often far easier to recognize this value in theoretical terms than it is when you are in power and being criticized, but that is why it is vital that politicians can take a mature, long-term view and focus on ensuring the conditions for healthy democracy, rather than simply making life easier for themselves in the short term.

If the pluralism rationale provides a solid basis for offering tax breaks on charitable donations, we are still faced with the question of implementation: what form should these tax breaks take and how can we ensure they are effective? In terms of form, there are two broad options: a tax deduction (where some or all of the value of donations is subtracted from the donor's taxable income prior to tax being calculated) or a tax credit (where some or all of the value of donations is given as a lump sum that can be used towards the donor's tax bill). The US – the most influential philanthropic market in the world – offers a charitable deduction, and deductions are more common than credits internationally. (An OECD report on tax and philanthropy found that of forty countries surveyed in depth, twenty-two offered deductions for charitable giving and twelve offered credits.)[22] There are also some anomalies, such as the UK, which offer a hybrid tax relief through the Gift Aid system, where basic rate tax relief comes in the form of a credit paid directly to the recipient charity, but higher-rate relief comes in the form of a tax deduction for the donor through self-assessment.

In general, deductions are seen as simpler to administer and easier to understand, but this may come at the cost of fairness because they produce an 'upside-down effect', where the value of the deduction is greater for wealthier people on higher incomes (as they would otherwise be paying a higher rate of tax). In the US, this is exacerbated by the fact that the charitable deduction is only available to those who file an itemized tax return, which is heavily correlated with home ownership (and thus higher incomes). Furthermore, there has always been a broader 'standard deduction' available to all taxpayers, which lumps charitable giving in with a host of other things. Recent years have seen the value of this rise significantly, offering an additional disincentive for most people to bother getting specific tax relief on their philanthropic giving. As a result, two economists calculated in 2019 that the percentage of taxpayers claiming the charitable deduction had fallen from the already-low level of around 25 per cent to only 8.5 per cent.[23]

This highlights the fact that the other challenge for any government offering tax relief on charitable giving is to ensure it is effective. Assessing whether something is effective, of course, depends on knowing what you are trying to achieve; in this case, is the primary purpose of offering tax relief to get more people giving (that is, to broaden the base of donors) or to get people giving more (to encourage those already making donations to maximize their value)? If it is the former, then low levels of take-up are clearly a major barrier to considering the incentive effective. If it is more the latter, however, we need to ascertain whether the incentives offered genuinely result in greater levels of giving. There is no conclusive economic evidence on this, but studies suggest that giving behaviour is inelastic in responses to changes in tax rate (that is, it doesn't have a significant impact), so we need to be careful not to overestimate the effect that tax has in getting people to give more. We also need to be wary of the risk that we are simply 'buying the base' by rewarding donation behaviour that would have happened anyway, which is unlikely to be seen as a good use of taxpayers' money. Perhaps, though, coming back to the pluralism rational we decided on above, the real value of offering tax incentives for giving is less about the specific amounts raised and more about the message it sends that governments recognize the importance of a healthy and diverse civil society. If that is the case, then it is up to each government to decide how much that messaging is worth to them and how that should be reflected in the value of any tax incentives offered for philanthropic giving.

5
PHILANTHROPY OR DEMOCRACY?

Philanthropic foundations are 'repugnant to the whole idea of a democratic society',[1] declared the Unitarian minister Reverend John Hayes Holmes when testifying before the Commission on Industrial Relations in the US Congress in 1912. Conversely, the 1952 Nathan Committee report in the UK argued that 'the democratic state as we know it could hardly function effectively or teach the exercise of democracy to its members without such channels for and demands upon voluntary service', and suggested that voluntary service should be seen as 'a nursery school of democracy'.[2] So which is it? Is philanthropy an anti-democratic menace that can bypass and subvert the will of the people? Or is it a vital component of any healthy democracy, helping to ensure pluralism and foster civic engagement? The answer, as we shall see, is not clear-cut, and raises challenging questions about whether all forms of giving should be considered equal, and what constraints we might need on the freedoms of donors to ensure that philanthropy is a positive force.

Does philanthropy weaken democracy?

One of the key charges levelled against philanthropy is that it is a means for the wealthy to bypass the machinery of representative democracy in order to shape public opinion and public policy, and thus introduces a 'plutocratic bias' into society. It was this concern that led Frank Walsh, the chairman of the Commission on Industrial Relations, to warn in 1915 that 'the huge philanthropic trusts known as foundations, appear to be a menace to the welfare of society'.[3] Unlike elected officials or politicians, philanthropists are not accountable to anyone. As political philosopher Rob Reich puts it, 'big philanthropy is often an unaccountable, non-transparent, donor-directed, and perpetual exercise of power. This is something that fits uneasily, at best, in democratic societies that enshrine the value of political equality.'[4]

The use of 'big' in this critique is noteworthy, as it makes clear that it is specifically aimed at the philanthropy of the elite rather than the giving of the average person (or even of those with relatively significant means). 'Non-transparent' is also important, as one of the key concerns in recent years – particularly in the US – is that philanthropy has become a route for deliberately opaque 'dark money' to make its way into public and political life, via a network of nonprofit

Figure 5.1: UK prime minister David Cameron and philanthropist Melinda French Gates with young people at the London Summit on Family Planning, 2012

Politicians like to engage with high-profile philanthropists. For the philanthropist, it's a chance to influence policy and debate on issues they care about. For the politician, it offers the promise of drawing in additional funding and perhaps adding an alluring sheen of celebrity to their work. Critics, however, raise concerns about the political influence that the wealthy can wield through philanthropy and ask whether this presents a challenge to democracy.

advocacy groups and think tanks. Many calls for reform in philanthropy have therefore centred around demands for greater transparency and openness.

Reich's use of 'perpetual' is also deliberate, as there is a particularly long-standing critique of the role of perpetual endowments in a democracy (structures which allow charitable money to be held for an indefinite period, with investment returns given out in grants). The criticism is that this results in injustice and unfairness because it allows wealthy individuals to enshrine their priorities and values in organizational form and thus not only exert influence during their lifetime, but for generations to come. This 'dead hand of the donor' is objectionable both as a matter of principle, it is argued, and for the practical reason that the longer an endowment exists, the higher the risk that its original founding purposes will come to look ill-focused or just plain wrong.

The French economist Anne-Robert-Jacques Turgot launched the first salvo in the war on perpetual endowments in the late eighteenth century, arguing that

> Public utility is the supreme law [and] must not be tempered with superstitious respect for the so-called intentions of the founders as if individuals, ignorant and limited as they are, have the right to subject unborn generations to their caprice ... Let us conclude that no work of man is made for eternity, and since foundations, continually multiplied by vanity would ultimately absorb all wealth and private property, we must be able to destroy them.[5]

The philosopher John Stuart Mill drew a slightly less dramatic conclusion in the nineteenth century, suggesting that, while endowments should perhaps not exist unchanged in perpetuity, there was a reasonable case for allowing them for a fixed term or during the lifetime of a donor on the grounds that this would allow plurality and experimentation within civil society.[6] However it was the nineteenth-century English judge Sir Arthur Hobhouse who really picked up the baton, becoming a prominent critic of perpetual endowments and even publishing a book entitled *The Dead Hand*.[7] Hobhouse argued that by allowing permanent endowments 'we have said that any man, however selfish or stupid, may assume to foresee the needs of all future time' and that we shouldn't be surprised if this led to problematic results, noting sardonically, 'what wonder if there is poverty of result from acts for the performance of which we require neither wisdom, nor public spirit, nor self-denial.'

Lending further weight to Hobhouse's arguments was the fact that by the mid-nineteenth century London was overrun with dormant parochial trusts. This became a *cause célèbre* for reform campaigners, who thought it morally unacceptable that at a time of great poverty so much money was locked up trusts with such

Figure 5.2: 'Vanity Beyond the Grave'. Engraving by N. Guérard, c. 1715

Death and concerns about legacy have long played a shaping role in philanthropy. Here, a wealthy man lies on his deathbed as his will, including a range of extravagant charitable bequests, is read. A poem below the image, 'Fashionable Wills and Joyful Mourning' (not shown), reads: 'All these bequests made at the end, We often make out of vanity. Close to God has no merit; Whoever wants to make a happy ending, Must leave it early on, To heaven and his neighbour'.

narrow and archaic purposes that the money in them could effectively never be spent. There was reportedly a trust for providing funds for killing ladybirds on Cornhill (a street in the City of London) and even a fund for buying bundles of wood for burning heretics (not something that was in great demand by the mid-Victorian period).[8]

Concerns about perpetuity gained new impetus in early twentieth-century America with the arrival of the great mega-foundations of the Gilded Age. Commenting on J.D. Rockefeller's plans to create an endowed foundation with his fortune, one newspaper warned that 'just as the enormous influence of the monasteries in the Middle Ages was based largely upon inalienable property and its usufruct [beneficial use], so these private incorporated foundations, living forever, would attain an influence anti-social and anti-democratic to an extraordinary degree'.[9] There were also donors who shared these concerns: the Sears & Roebuck CEO Julius Rosenwald, who was a noted philanthropist in his own right, made it clear that he was 'opposed to gifts in perpetuity for any purpose' because 'whilst charity tends to do good, perpetual charities tend to do evil'.[10] His contemporary, the photography pioneer and manufacturer George Eastman, meanwhile, offered perhaps the pithiest critique of perpetuity when he declared that in his opinion 'men who leave their money to be distributed by others are pie-face mutts'.[11] Both Rosenwald and Eastman practised what they preached by ensuring that their own foundations were established with a limited life-span (which perhaps accounts for them being less well known than some of the other philanthropists whose names are still carried by major foundations).

Debates over perpetuity and the time horizons of philanthropy are raging still. Defenders of perpetual endowments argue that they enable philanthropy to take a long-term view, a vital strength at a time when political and economic cycles have become increasingly short-term. Critics, however, continue to highlight concerns about the dead hand of the donor, arguing that perpetual endowments heighten the potentially anti-democratic nature of philanthropy and undermine its claims to be a tool for furthering justice. These arguments have gained greater intensity in recent times as the need to respond to the scale of challenges like the COVID-19 pandemic and the climate crisis has led to calls for a higher proportion of foundation resources to be deployed far more quickly, including assets currently tied up in perpetual endowments. At the same time, a new generation of donors with a greater thirst for immediacy is emerging. This has led to more emphasis on the idea of 'giving while living' popularized by the Irish-American billionaire Chuck Feeney, who decided in 2002 to spend out all the remaining money in his Atlantic Philanthropies foundation over the coming twenty years (which he did: the organization shut its doors as planned in 2022). The adoption by a new generation of donors of a similar approach will almost certainly lend further weight to arguments against perpetuity as a default.

5.1 Thought experiment: Set up a foundation, or spend it all now?

You have just sold a successful start-up and you are thinking about using most of the profits to get involved in philanthropy. You speak to two friends who have been big givers for a long time to get their advice. One friend suggests giving all of the money away now to a range of charities already working in your local area to address pressing needs such as homelessness and poverty. The other friend suggests setting up an endowed foundation so that you can give over the longer term out of the investment returns.

Which do you do? Is it better simply to support the work of existing charities working on issues that are clearly pressing and could use your money now? Or is there an argument for setting up a vehicle that allows you to distribute money over a longer period? If so, should it still have a finite lifespan? And how long is long enough?

Another concern is that philanthropy can shackle democracy by stifling the dissent that is often necessary for more radical change to occur. Elites, it is argued, can use their giving as a means of social control, staving off unrest by providing a salve or distraction that does just enough to keep the populace subdued but does nothing to challenge the status quo. This is a suspicion with a rich history; indeed, W.K. Jordan suggests that from the very outset of the modern era of philanthropy at the turn of the seventeenth century 'the Tudors viewed charity as a necessary aspect of public policy rather than as a requirement of Christian morality' precisely because that charity could meet the needs of the poor and thereby address the fact that 'unrelieved, uncontrolled want constituted a grave threat to the stability of the realm'.[12] Subduing unrest was not necessarily always a conscious aim of giving since, as historian Frank Prochaska notes, 'the ruling classes largely took it for granted that deference would flow from their philanthropy'.[13] However, during times of particular social tension – such as wars, famines or epidemics – recognition that charity could play an important role in maintaining the fabric of society became more explicit. An 1881 newspaper editorial even argued that benevolence helped 'crush out that class feeling which at times threatens to turn this England of ours into two hostile camps'.[14]

Many wealthy individuals throughout the nineteenth and early twentieth centuries harboured ongoing fears that gross inequality and growing working-class identity would lead to the toppling of existing structures of capitalism that had made them rich. They therefore saw their philanthropy in part as 'riot insurance', or as Ben Whitaker puts it, 'Danegeld [a tax] that must be paid to preserve capitalism and to contain discontent lest it breed subversion and revolution'.[15] Labour activists were fully alive to this role of philanthropy and often made it the focus of their criticism. The women's rights campaigner Florence Kelley dismissed elite giving as 'a means by which capitalists return to the workers a small fraction of the wealth stolen from them in order to control "the dependent and dangerous classes" and avert the revolution.'[16] Others, meanwhile, used this tension to their advantage. The charity leader Thomas Barnardo, a canny but not always entirely scrupulous fundraiser, was perfectly willing to play on fears of unrest to drum up more support for his work with orphans, declaring that 'every boy rescued from the gutter is one dangerous man the less' and that if nothing was done 'this seething mass of human misery will shake the social fabric'.[17]

Today, philanthropy may be a less reliable tool for purchasing deference. However, there are still many critics who accuse big donors of engaging in a 'bread and circuses' approach, where their giving is done with an eye to staving off criticism of themselves and the capitalist system in which they have prospered. Philanthropic foundations, too, may be part of the problem here if they follow the template set by Henry Ford II, who argued that a foundation is essentially 'a creature of capitalism' and that every foundation therefore has 'obligations to our economic system' and should consider how 'as one of the system's most prominent offspring [it] might act most wisely to strengthen and improve its progenitor.'[18] Foundations might not consciously see the defence of a capitalist status quo as part of their role, but if the range of activities they are willing to support is constrained too far by fear of funding anything too radical, it may well amount to the same thing. This has been a particular concern when foundations engage with social movements – as happened during the 1960s and 1970s with civil rights and Black power movements and is happening again today, according to philanthropy scholars Megan Ming Francis and Erica Kohl Arenas, with Black Lives Matter – because often, simply by the choices they make about what to fund or the restrictions they place on what count as 'acceptable' activities, foundations can 'tame' or co-opt movements.[19] In doing so the danger is that, even if the engagement is well-intentioned, philanthropy once again become a means to suppress dissent and thereby undermines democracy.

Plurality, discovery and innovation

Contrary to the critiques we have considered so far, many would argue that far from undermining democracy, philanthropy plays a key role in strengthening it. A key attribute often identified is philanthropy's role in fostering greater plurality by supporting a diverse civil society that provides space for a wide range of ideas and values to be expressed outside of the ambit of the state. This is good, proponents suggest, as electoral democracy on its own always carries with it the risk of a 'tyranny of the majority'. Members of minority groups or those with minority views may be prevented from expressing their choices in any meaningful way through standard democratic means (either representative or direct), simply because they lack the necessary numbers. While this remains 'democratic' in a strict sense, it is flawed if it results in an unjust treatment of those in the minority when left unchecked.

Civil society can offer an important counterbalance by allowing people to exert influence collectively, even though they may remain firmly in the minority within society as a whole. The historian R.J. Morris notes that 'one major contribution which the voluntary association has made to ordering the complexities of urban and industrial society has been its contribution to the history of "out-groups": groups which were excluded from a significant share in the legitimate structure of power.'[20] So charitable organizations have often played a vital role by giving those in marginalized communities a means of finding and asserting their shared identity, which has in many cases resulted in a change in their fortunes within society over the longer term.

The argument in favour of philanthropy here is predicated on the value of plurality and free association, and the role they can play in decentralizing power and public choice within a system that might otherwise be highly centralized. Should we be wary, however, of the concentration of power and resources in certain organizations within civil society leading to a recentralization, but outside the reach of the state and the norms of democratic accountability? The founding fathers of the US thought so, and saw formal voluntary organizations as a potential risk to their fledgling democracy precisely because they might enable factions to form, which could then become power bases outside of government. President George Washington even used his farewell address in 1796 to warn that voluntary associations 'serve to organize faction, and put in place of the delegated will of the Nation the will of a small but artful and enterprising minority of the community', so that over time they would become 'potent engines, by which cunning, ambitious and unprincipled men will be able to subvert the Power of the People'.[21]

Similar concerns were heard throughout the nineteenth century in the US. In 1828, the leader of Boston Unitarianism, William Ellery Channing, argued that formalized civil society organizations

> accumulate power in a few hands, and this takes place just in proportion to the surface over which they spread. In a large institution, a few men rule, a few do everything; and if the institution happens to be directed at objects about which conflict and controversy exist, a few are able to excite in the mass strong and bitter passions, and by these to obtain an immense ascendancy.[22]

Washington and Channing were primarily concerned about the leaders of organizations, but the same arguments could equally be applied to any philanthropists funding them. If an organization or cause has little backing in terms of the numbers of supporters, but can call upon major financial resources from one or more big donors, what should we make of this? On the one hand, we have seen that a key argument in favour of philanthropy as a positive force in a democracy is precisely that it can go against the grain and support causes or ideas that have little public support. The philosopher John Stuart Mill argued that philanthropic endowments could act as a 'precious safeguard for uncustomary modes of thought and practice',[23] and the social reformer Thomas Hare pointed out that 'the most important steps in human progress may be opposed to the prejudices not only of the multitudes, but even of the learned and leaders of thought in a particular era'.[24] Likewise, the economist Friedrich Hayek declared that 'public opinion cannot decide in what direction efforts should be made to arouse public opinion', so 'efforts have to be set in motion by a few individuals who possess the necessary resources themselves or win the support of those that do.'[25]

On the other hand, allowing elite donors to use their financial resources to support and spread views that reflect their own interests and can be used to shape public discourse and policymaking, even if they enjoy little support among the wider public, seems profoundly anti-democratic. This is an extremely difficult tension to resolve, not helped by the fact that we tend to draw different conclusions depending on whether we agree with the aims of the philanthropist in question. As philanthropy journalist David Callahan notes:

> When donors hold views we detest, we tend to see them as unfairly tilting policy debates with their money. Yet when we like their causes, we often view them as heroically stepping forward to level the playing field against powerful special interests or backward public majorities.[26]

So those towards the progressive end of the political spectrum are likely to be far less sanguine about the Koch brothers donating millions of dollars to organizations that promote climate change denial than they are about George Soros donating similar amounts to promote liberal democracy around the world (and vice versa).

5.2 Thought experiment: The price of philanthropic plurality?

You are a philanthropist focusing on climate issues. The government of your country has introduced new laws and policies that increasingly make it difficult for civil society organizations to speak out on issues it deems 'political'. You are contacted by an organization you suspect has accepted funding from the fossil fuel lobby to downplay the threat of climate change and slow the implementation of 'zero carbon'. They propose joining forces to lobby in favour of protecting civil society freedoms, on the basis that they are equally important to both of you.

What do you do? Should you partner up with this organization to defend the freedom of philanthropists to fund advocacy and campaigning work, despite the fact you disagree on every substantive issue? Or are you happy to accept strict limitations on your own freedom to support efforts to address the climate crisis if it means they are no longer able to support climate change denial?

Of course, this makes little sense if we are trying to find a universal answer to the question of how much freedom we should afford to philanthropists to advance their own views about what would make for a better society. In many ways the more useful thought experiment is to take the least palatable example of currently allowable philanthropy that you can come up with and ask whether you are willing to accept that as the cost of plurality. Am I, for instance, happy to accept that some donors should be free to fund climate scepticism as the price for preserving the freedom for other donors to fund causes I do agree with? Or should I try to argue that climate scepticism is not a legitimate cause for philanthropy in an objective sense (in the knowledge that others may try to mount similar arguments against causes I think should be allowed)? The answer to this may rest in part on whether we believe that the spread of resources in support of different viewpoints would be well-balanced if philanthropy was left to its own devices. And there is reason to suspect this is unlikely in practice because research suggests that the very wealthy tend to have views that are more conservative that society as a whole; so big-money philanthropy is likely to skew in favour of certain viewpoints.[27] Perhaps, then, we cannot afford to be so sanguine about allowing philanthropy free rein in the 'battle of ideas'. But if the alternative is to constrain the freedom for philanthropy to fund unpopular causes and support minority views, how do we do that without losing the value of the role it has played as a check on the tyranny of the majority? As Warren Weaver, the long-time director of the Rockefeller Foundation's Natural Sciences Division, put it in 1954:

> If we believe in democracy and in the right to express dissenting ideas, a small amount of pathology must be tolerated in order to maintain the health of the main social body, somewhat as protective antibodies are produced in the human body by injecting small amounts of material associated with disease. The edge of desirable experimentation must continuously be tested with vigour and variety, and can be located only by occasionally crossing it. We accept a small risk to make a large gain.[28]

We saw in Chapter 3 that philanthropy has often played a key role in taking issues from the margins to the mainstream by building awareness and support that has eventually led to major milestones in social progress. There are many examples of this, from the abolition of slavery and the ending of child labour, to universal suffrage and the decriminalization of homosexuality. And in every case, the role of philanthropic support as a means of overcoming the tyranny of the majority has been vital, particularly in the early stages where an issue has little public awareness or support. That is why the freedom for individuals to run counter to the status quo by supporting marginal causes, and the freedom for civil society organizations to campaign and speak out on issues remain so important. Through campaigning and advocacy work, research, network-building, organizing protests and a host of other means, these organizations highlight new challenges and unmet needs, bring issues to public attention and challenge governments when they fail to meet citizens' requirements and expectations. By doing so they act as a crucial mechanism for holding those in power to account, one which is just as important and legitimate as the ballot box, and as such they are a vital part of maintaining a healthy and responsive democracy. That is why it is such a concern that in many countries around the world the freedoms that civil society organizations need in order to play this role – freedoms of speech, protest and association – are being deliberately eroded. If the phenomenon of closing space for civil society continues, democracy will suffer.

Elite philanthropy may be hard to justify based on plurality alone if, in practice, the ideas and approaches it supports skew towards the interests and values of the wealthy. However, the role of big giving within a democracy may still be justifiable if it can be argued that those ideas and approaches help to drive experimentation and innovation that benefit society (even if they are not genuinely pluralistic). Political philosopher Rob Reich argues that 'discovery' is in fact the most compelling basis for the legitimacy of elite philanthropy and foundations in a democracy because they 'can serve as democratic society's "risk capital", a potent discovery mechanism for experimentation in social policy with uncertain results over the long term.'[29] This innovation might take the form of finding new ways to do things that the state already does, but it might also mean demonstrating new things that the state should be doing.

One might ask why we need philanthropy to perform this function. Surely the state could experiment and innovate on its own? It is certainly true that there is plenty of focus on the notion of innovation within the public sector around the world and conversely that the public sector has played a key (but often underappreciated) role in enabling innovation in many areas of the private sector by supporting early stage research and development work (as detailed by the economist Mariana Mazzucato).[30] However, advocates of the innovation role of philanthropy would argue that too often the state is risk-averse and unwilling to try new things. Bill Gates, for instance, has suggested that philanthropy 'is there because the government is not very innovative, doesn't try risky things'.[31] If this is true, then a key part of philanthropy's strength when it comes to innovation is that it is more willing to take risks than the state.

But why would this be the case? One reason is that philanthropy may be better able to take a long-term view. We have seen that longevity has sometimes been a source of criticism, due to concerns about perpetuity and the dead hand of the donor, but the flip side is that working over a longer time horizon can allow philanthropic funders to test approaches that may not deliver measurable outcomes until much further down the line, which is often not possible in the public sector because short-term political cycles demand immediate results. Another reason that philanthropy may be more able to take risks is its lack of accountability. Those working in government or the public sector are

– directly or indirectly – accountable to voters; but philanthropic foundations are only accountable to a board of trustees, and individual philanthropists are fundamentally accountable to no one but themselves. This has again been a source of criticism, as some feel this lack of accountability makes philanthropy anti-democratic. However, it is also this same lack of accountability which makes it possible to take risks and invest in innovation that might benefit society, because there are no angry shareholders or taxpayers to take issue if an experiment fails.

It seems, then, as though risk-taking might be one of philanthropy's core strengths. Indeed, the secretary of the Carnegie UK Trust declared back in 1952 that 'it is the business of trusts to live dangerously'.[32] This raises two immediate questions: firstly, does this mean that *all* philanthropy must be risk-taking and innovative, or merely a certain proportion of it (so that it is still OK for some philanthropy to fund tried-and-tested or low-risk activities)? And secondly, how much philanthropy in practice meets this criterion of driving discovery? Are big-ticket philanthropists and foundations genuinely pursuing innovative goals or using innovative methods, or are many of them simply playing it safe? It is clearly hard to assess this in any systematic way, in part because the information we would require about the overall distribution of philanthropy is not available, and also because what counts as successful innovation is subjective. However, the charge of being unimaginative or risk-averse is certainly levelled at philanthropy from time to time.

Even during the supposed Victorian golden age of philanthropy in the UK, for example, critics argued that the scale of giving masked the fact that a large majority of it was extremely conservative. Historian David Owen notes that

> the chief impression left by late-century bequests is not that of eccentricity but that of conventionality ... few contained anything particularly venturesome or imaginative. Money went, on the whole, to maintain established institutions or to create new ones of the same sort.[33]

As well as failing to be innovative enough, can philanthropy also be too innovative? At what point, for instance, does a 'philanthropic big bet' become a wild goose chase or a vanity project that misdirects resources? These are pertinent questions at a time when a growing number of big donors (particularly those from Silicon Valley) are choosing to focus their philanthropy on issues such as human space exploration or countering 'existential risks' like AI takeover (the hypothetical point at which an artificial intelligence develops beyond human capability and starts running the show). Some would argue that these are precisely the sort of long-term big issues that should be the focus of philanthropy, and that given the lack of progress we have made in human space travel since the 1970s, and the possibility that our future as a species depends on expansion to the stars, a focus on space exploration might well represent the best possible use of philanthropic resources. Others, however, argue that this sort of philanthropy is little more than an ego trip for billionaires who have made a lot of money from technology and thus naturally see the world through a technocentric lens.

In practical terms, the question is whether anything can be done to rein in the tendency of some philanthropists to go off on quixotic tangents and get them to focus instead on the immediate and pressing needs in the world right now; but without constraining the freedom of donors to the point where they decide to stop giving. Rob Reich proposes we could adopt something akin to the system of academic peer review; so the schemes of a given philanthropist would be subject to the approval of a body of their relevant peers, who could then determine whether or not that approach should be seen as legitimate. In this way, Reich argues, 'peer review could in principle foster norms that, without the need for formal legal regulation, help to hold private foundations to a discovery mode.'[34]

There are a number of obvious challenges with this: the first is that getting philanthropists – who are often very individualistic and idealistic – to accept any given group of people as their peers when it comes to assessing their giving might be a tall order. Conversely, even if you could get philanthropists to agree to this kind of scrutiny, there might be a danger that groupthink and confirmation bias within their peer group would simply result in everyone agreeing that their philanthropic goals were the right ones. There is also the issue that judging the value of philanthropic big bets is often far easier in hindsight than it is ahead of time, so, by making philanthropy beholden to peer review, would we simply be reducing its capacity for experimentation and innovation?

Voluntary action as 'a nursery of democracy'?

It may not be the outcomes of philanthropy or voluntary action that are most valuable when it comes to strengthening democracy, but rather the process of producing them, if this teaches people vital skills of citizenship and democratic participation. This idea stems from eighteenth-century political philosopher Alexis de Tocqueville, who argued that voluntary action can act as a 'nursery of democracy'. This is arguably the case even if the causes that people engage with have little or nothing to do with citizenship or democracy. According to sociologist Robert Putnam, 'these effects do not require that the manifest purpose of the association be political ... taking part in a choral society or a bird-watching club can teach self-discipline and an appreciation for the joys of successful collaboration.'[35]

These democratic benefits of voluntary action have been appreciated across the political spectrum. On the right, they have traditionally been associated with a desire to minimize the size of the state and a focus on individual agency and responsibility. Hence in a pamphlet for the right-leaning UK think tank Civitas, historian Frank Prochaska wrote approvingly of the way that 'associational philanthropy carries forward the ancient obligation of civic duty within a commercial society, with its accent on individual autonomy' and lauded philanthropic bodies as 'bastions of democratic pluralism, an expression of both the rights and duties of republican citizenship.'[36]

Conversely, historians Justin Davis Smith and Melanie Oppenheimer note that 'the role of voluntary action as a training ground for future labour leaders' was 'an equally strong tradition within the British labour movement.'[37] Many key figures of twentieth-century Labour and Liberal politics such as Clement Attlee and William Beveridge had formative experiences working in university settlements and 'this early exposure to the principles and values of voluntary action clearly influenced their future thinking on the proper balance to be struck between the state and voluntary endeavour.' Likewise, the left-leaning social scientist Constance Braithwaite argued in her 1938 book *The Voluntary Citizen* that 'the qualities of citizenship desirable in the democratic community of the future are far more likely to be developed by ... active participation in the work of voluntary associations ... than by methods of mass propaganda and deification of the State.'[38]

This role of philanthropy and voluntary action as a means of learning skills of citizenship and a route into the wider democratic system has often proved particularly important for groups excluded from the mainstream political system or public life. During the nineteenth century, the involvement of both middle- and working-class women in charity work played a key role in paving the way for the fight for universal suffrage that was to come. Many women started out focusing on traditional areas of charity rather than on campaigning for their right to vote, but as Prochaska argues, over time 'the interest of philanthropic women in female suffrage emerged quite naturally out of certain of their activities, for as the more penetrating of them argued, there were limits to their freedom of action without political power.'[39] At the same time, involvement in voluntary associations taught these women many skills and tactics that were to prove crucial for their later suffrage efforts. At the start of the nineteenth century it was almost unheard of for women to speak in public and it was only through the efforts of many women 'determined to get their message across and willing to test convention by addressing charity meetings, social science congresses, and trade union gatherings'[40] that this changed over the course of the century, so that by the time the suffragette movement was in full swing it was at least possible for them to get their voices heard (even if not always listened to). Historian Kathleen McCarthy traces a similar story in the US, where

> for nonpoliticized American women, giving and voluntarism have provided ongoing sources of recruitment, socialization, training and advancement into public roles ... [and] have also provided the crucibles in which women have reshaped public policies and popular attitudes about gender, class, domesticity and race.[41]

There are those, however, who urge caution about taking too rose-tinted a view of voluntary action as a nursery of democracy. Some point out that philanthropic organizations are not always themselves especially democratic and that historically many of them represented explicit attempts to reinforce existing hierarchies and power dynamics rather than bring marginalized groups into the fold of mainstream democracy. According to historian R.J. Morris, in the nineteenth century

> the leaders of the dominant voluntary societies felt that they were engaged in the creation of a particular set of social relationships which were intended to provide stability and legitimacy for their own power and privilege ... the end product of this process was intended to be a society of independent, hard-working, self-disciplined owners of small units of property, created and directed by an elite which still concentrated wealth and power in their own hands.[42]

Other critics, meanwhile, argue that the skills learned through participating in single issue, caused-based organizations may not actually be that useful to wider democratic engagement. Historian Brian Harrison suggests that in fact 'preoccupation with a single issue encourages black-and-white views of the world which readily dismiss difference of opinion as devious, malicious or corrupt. In this situation, the voluntarist promotes not democratic political education but an over-fastidious half-retreat from the real world.'[43]

Some critics also question whether we should be so ready to consider voluntary associations as positive forces for fostering democracy regardless of their actual purpose. The political scientist Joan Roelofs points out that the nonprofit sector in the US includes 'the Ku Klux Klan, militias, Black Panthers, pacifists, exclusive country clubs, city clubs, foreign relations think tanks, fundamentalist religions of many denominations and a variety of others' and that 'these inconvenient denizens are rarely, if ever, discussed'.[44] The emergence in recent years of a proliferation of new far-right groups and networks in the US, many of which are contemptuous of electoral democracy and some of which even played a role in the attack on the US Capitol building on 6 January 2021, has sharpened these concerns further. It is certainly difficult to see how participation in a group that actively wants to undermine the electoral system and the rule of law can be anything other than a threat to democracy. Thus we need to distinguish more carefully between different types of civil society organizations when making a case for their value in fostering civic engagement and skills of citizenship.

Does philanthropy itself need to be more democratic?

Given the arguments we have just considered, is it possible to maximize philanthropy's potential as a positive force within a democracy, while minimizing the anti-democratic risk it poses? And what changes might this require us to make?

When it comes to plutocratic bias, one solution may be to look for models that push big donors towards developing grassroots support rather than going it alone. This may be simply by working through existing organizations that can call on a wider support base, so that any philanthropic funding does not have a disproportionate effect. Or it may be by using philanthropic resources to encourage a wider culture of giving at a more modest, everyday level, in the hope that this helps to ensure genuine plurality within civil society.

When it comes to intergenerational injustice caused by perpetual endowments and the 'dead hand', some would argue that the only solution is to make all philanthropic foundations time-limited or 'spend-down' (required to use up all of their capital over a given period, rather than simply using the investment returns from an endowment that can in theory exist in perpetuity). However, others urge caution that we should not lose sight of the value that longer time horizons may bring by enabling philanthropy to play a role in supporting innovation. A potential compromise might be to shift from a default norm of perpetuity for foundations to one of limited lifespans; so that long-term or perpetual structures are still allowable, but the exception.

Cutting across many of the concerns we have explored is the question of how power is distributed within philanthropy. An important part of addressing them is for philanthropic funders to find ways of giving away power as well as money. This may be as simple as shifting from a norm of programmatic, restricted funding to one of unrestricted funding for core costs, which a growing number of philanthropic funders are exploring and which is almost always identified by recipient organizations as the number-one measure that would help to empower them more. Other funders are going even further and experimenting with participatory methods for some or all of their grantmaking. These approaches range widely in terms of how much participation they involve, but their common element is that they bring the people and communities who would once have been seen as the passive recipients of philanthropy into active decision-making about where resources should be allocated.

5.3 Thought experiment: Lived experience vs expertise

You're a philanthropist who has been supporting medical research and treatment addressing a narrow range of childhood illnesses for more than thirty years. You've been making efforts to shift towards a participatory grantmaking approach, in which those suffering from illnesses (and their families) have a greater say over how resources are distributed. A dispute has recently broken out between some of the families involved in the participatory grantmaking process and the staff of your foundation about what money should be spent on.

The families claim that their lived experience is being ignored and that they should just be given the money to spend according to their own assessment of their needs. The foundation staff, meanwhile, argue that their professional expertise is being ignored, and that some of the suggestions for how the money should be spent would be at best ineffective, and at worst actively harmful.

How should you resolve this tension? Is lived experience on a par with professional expertise, or should we weigh one above the other? How do you decide on the appropriate balance if so? If you decide to give recipients full freedom and they choose to spend money in ways you disagree with, should you impose more constraints? Or is this just a potential cost of rebalancing power within philanthropy?

It is also vital that philanthropic funders recognize and support the value of civil society advocacy and campaigning, and join efforts to protect them against repressive government policies that seek to stifle fundamental rights of free speech, protest and association. In a polarized climate where proponents of culture war narratives have deliberately redrawn the boundaries of what is deemed controversial or 'political', philanthropists may be wary of taking a stand if they fear it will make them the subject of partisan attacks. However, the freedoms on which civil society rests are fragile and we may find that if we don't protect them, the longer-term cost to our democracy could be enormous.

6

PHILANTHROPY
OR THE MARKET?

'It is not from the benevolence of the butcher, the brewer, or the baker, that we expect our dinner, but from their regard to their own interest', wrote the eighteen-century economist Adam Smith; 'we address ourselves, not to their humanity but to their self-love, and never talk to them of our own necessities but of their advantages.'[1] According to this view, the free market and philanthropy are fundamentally different, both in the effects they produce and the motivations that drive them, and the market is a superior basis on which to run a society. In reality, the lines between altruism and economic self-interest are often far blurrier than we might think. Recent years, for instance, have seen a huge surge of interest in 'impact investment' and 'social business' approaches that combine profit with purpose.

Proponents claim these offer an alternative to our traditional models of philanthropy and will play a key role in addressing social and environmental challenges in the future. This may well be so, but it is not in fact a particularly new idea. Throughout the ages people have sought to bridge the divide between doing good and making money by making charity more 'businesslike', and conversely by making business more charitable. So how should we understand the relationship between philanthropy and the market?

Making charity more 'businesslike'

A common refrain among those who want to reform philanthropy is that donors and charitable organizations simply need to become more businesslike. This is a core part of the doctrine of 'philanthrocapitalism', first characterized in a 2008 book by Matthew Bishop and Michael Green, whose original subtitle, 'how the rich can save the world and why we should let them', perhaps now seems overly bullish in light of the critiques of philanthropy in recent years, but whose core ideas continue to be influential.[2] But what does it mean in practice for philanthropy to become more businesslike?

One interpretation is that the models of governance and administration in philanthropic organizations should more closely mirror those of commercial enterprises. There is some historical logic to this, as modern charities have their roots in the 'associated philanthropy' that arose in the seventeenth and eighteenth centuries and were in part based on the model of the joint stock company, which became commonplace in the same period due to the proliferation of new enterprises during the industrial revolution. Whereas before, giving had been primarily an individual, person-to-person affair, now multiple donors could pool resources and create an organization to manage their distribution, in the same way that multiple shareholders could take stakes in a business. Over time, of course, the commercial and charitable spheres developed along different paths, so to suggest that charities merely needed to copy businesses became increasingly reductive (although that has not stopped people). More common from the nineteenth century was the idea that even if charities were not necessarily the same as businesses, they certainly needed to involve businesspeople if they were to succeed. The Liverpool philanthropist William Rathbone wrote in 1865 that 'charity has been an affair of sentiment rather than of principle; it has been left to impulsive enthusiasts instead of being recognized as a proper sphere for men of business habits and methodical minds.'[3] In many cases, however, the imposition of a business mindset may have had less to do with a deliberate vision for improving charity administration and more to do with the fact that 'voluntary charities were an expression of middle class culture', according to historian Peter Shapely, so 'those involved could be seen to have simply transposed their knowledge of administering a business organisation onto the structure of the voluntary charity.'[4]

Either way, not everyone has always bought in to the idea that businesspeople have some unique and semi-mystical expertise to bring to philanthropy. The sociologist Thorstein Veblen thought it merely reflected 'a sentimental conviction that pecuniary success is the final test of manhood' and that 'business principles are the sacred articles of the secular creed' while 'business methods make up the ritual of the secular cult.'[5] The philanthropist Julius Rosenwald, himself a highly successful businessman, went as far as to say that he 'could never understand the popular belief that because a man makes a lot of money he has a lot of brains', and that in fact 'some very rich men who made their own fortunes have been among the stupidest men I have ever met in my life.'[6]

Modern day critics such as Michael Edwards and Phil Buchanan continue to argue against the deification of business thinking. Edwards, a former Ford Foundation executive, argues that philanthrocapitalism 'sees business methods as the answer to social problems, but offers little rigorous evidence or analysis to support this claim, and ignores strong evidence pointing in the opposite direction'.[7] Buchanan, the founder of the Center for Effective Philanthropy, similarly argues that 'there is real danger that an appreciation of the nonprofit sector's distinctive identity and purpose will be lost if donors and nonprofit leaders look simplistically and misguidedly to the markets and "business practice" as the answers.'[8]

Even if unsolicited advice from businesspeople is not always appreciated, charitable organizations have certainly not been shy about adopting commercial approaches, particularly when it comes to raising money. The history of fundraising is one of constant innovation, in which charities have often been quick to take advantage of new technologies and new developments in the business world, and in some cases have even paved the way for businesses to follow. Charities, for instance, were quick to spot the value of entertainment and celebrity; as far back as 1750 George Frederick Handel donated an organ to London's Foundling Hospital on which he gave a recital of *Messiah* that raised £728, and subsequently left the original score to the charity in his will too.[9] In the nineteenth century, this kind of celebrity fundraising exploded, as theatre and music hall performances (and later sporting events) took place throughout the UK and the US to raise funds for charities. The Swedish singing sensation Jenny Lind spent so much time raising money for good causes with her shows that even her manager, the deeply cynical P.T. Barnum, was moved to exclaim that 'a visit from such a woman, who regards her artistic powers as a gift from Heaven for the amelioration of affliction and distress, and whose every thought and deed is philanthropy, I feel persuaded will prove a blessing to America'.[10]

Charities were also not afraid to tap into growing consumerism. In the eighteenth century, the renowned potter Josiah Wedgwood designed medallions to be sold by the Anti-Slavery Society to raise funds for their work[11] and in the following century the 'charity bazaar' (an early form of bring-and-buy sale) became a staple of the social landscape and a major money-spinner for charities.[12] Perhaps the canniest operator when it came to the commercialization of fundraising, though, was the Salvation Army founder 'General' William Booth, who was unashamed about milking newfound Victorian enthusiasm for purchasing. He often used his own fame as a draw, releasing early phonograph recordings of his speeches, as well as putting his face and name to all manner of products from decorative plates to car tyres. More intriguingly, the Salvation Army even released its own brand of 'Lights in Darkest England' safety matches (echoing the title of one of Booth's best-known books). These were in part designed as a money-making venture, but were also intended to promote the idea of 'ethical consumption' by offering an alternative to brands produced by young match-girls working in grim factory conditions and suffering the hideous effects of 'phossy jaw' as a result of exposure to white phosphorus.[13]

As the professionalization and commercialization of charities grew, so too, inevitably, did the complaints. *The Times* complained in 1880 that over-zealous fundraising meant that 'when a name has once been printed on a subscription list, its owner becomes a marked man ... from that day forward his persecution will never cease'.[14] Another newspaper bemoaned in 1892 the number of charity dance events and declared sternly that any charities relying on 'indirect crooked ways of catering for amusements' to raise money, rather than the strength of their cause, were destined to get their comeuppance eventually.[15] The criticism made its way into politics too: the Liberal MP E.H. Bayley led a one-man crusade against the Royal National Lifeboat

Institution in the 1890s, noting the 'extravagant salaries paid to the officials' and the large sums 'accumulating interest in the coffers of the institution'.[16] And looking back historically, Brian Harrison suggests that

> the numerous charity balls, philanthropic dinners and *conversaziones*, the pretentious central offices, the pages of print devoted to lists of subscriptions, the elegant membership cards ... all ensured that such redistribution of the national income as did take place in the nineteenth century gave pleasure to and even financially profited many of the not-so-poor before it finally filtered down to those in real need.[17]

Complaints about excessive salaries or wasteful spending continue to dog charities today. This is partly because the tools we have for measuring the value of charitable work remain limited, so donors often have only crude and unhelpful figures like the percentage spent on 'overheads' or 'administrative costs' to go on, even though these bear little or no relation to the actual effectiveness or impact of an organization. (Some highly effective charities may spend a relatively large amount on things that could be perceived as administration but are in fact vital core costs, while other charities could spend next to nothing on administration and yet be entirely ineffective. Which is better?) Yet at the same time charities often find themselves being criticized for not being 'professional' or 'businesslike' enough. This leaves many in an impossible position, knowing that they will be damned if they do spend money to make sure their fundraising and operations are run properly, but also damned if they don't.

Combining profit and purpose

Sometimes the ambition to bridge the gap between philanthropy and business has gone beyond trying to impose a businesslike approach on charity after the fact and focused instead on combining financial and social goals from the outset. Often this has meant replacing straightforward gifts with loans and other financial tools that involve some form of reimbursement for the donor (albeit usually at a lower rate than in a straightforward commercial transaction). As far back as the first century AD, Pliny the Younger was concocting complicated deals that involved donating some of his land to the state and then renting it back from them as a means of giving money for public uses while ensuring that the land remained properly managed and the money was not 'misdirected'.[18] Fast forward to 1361, and on his death from the plague Bishop Michael Northburgh left one thousand marks of silver to establish a fund that would make zero-interest, one-year loans on pawned objects.[19] A number of other 'loan charities' appeared over the following centuries, such as the one specified in the will of Sir Thomas White in the sixteenth century, which gave out the profits from his property holdings to twenty-four city corporations around the UK every twenty-four years for them to use in making interest-free loans to 'young freemen, preferable clothiers'.[20]

A recurring theme with these organizations was that over time they were often criticized for being too commercial; the desire to minimize the risk of bad loans resulted in money going to affluent members of the middle class rather than to the genuinely needy as originally intended. The culmination of these concerns came with the Charitable Corporation for Relief of the Industrious Poor, incorporated by royal charter in 1707, which existed to provide affordable loans to those who would otherwise be prey to unscrupulous pawnbrokers and usurers. The Charitable Corporation, as it became known, was viewed with suspicion from the outset by many who derided its shareholders as '10 per cent philanthropists', and unfortunately the management of the organization quickly lived down to these low expectations, with one director reportedly saying 'damn the poor, let us go into the City where we may get money'. Through a combination of mismanagement and outright fraud, the Corporation eventually collapsed, leaving the government to bail out its many unfortunate customers, and it was said that 'the circumstances under which it came to an end left a feeling of strong suspicion against this form of charity'.[21]

The notion of social lending historically enjoyed more success outside the UK. Late medieval Italy saw the emergence of *monti de pietà* (literally 'mounts of piety'), institutions that acted as 'a cross between charitable giving and an early version of a pawnbroker and a mutual bank', taking donations from wealthy individuals, guilds and other bodies and using them to make secured, low-interest loans to the working

Figure 6.1: Lithograph depicting various aspects of charity, philanthropy and poverty on the streets of Paris. By Villain, after Nicolas-Toussaint Charlet, 1840

A workman brings a starving Parisian family a bowl of soup while a banker from a 'Philanthropic bank' ignores them. On the wall of the bank are advertisements for books advocating the value of self-help and commercialism. This nineteenth-century image suggests punitive views of poverty and attempts to combine profit and purpose can lead to clearly uncharitable acts.

poor.[22] The model was so successful it spread across continental Europe to both Catholic and Protestant countries, and some of the *monti* continued to operate into the twentieth century.

Similarly, the US in the late nineteenth century saw the creation of a number of part socially motivated loan companies, such as the Providential Loan Company of New York, which was established in 1893 by a group of wealthy businessman including J.P. Morgan and Cornelius Vanderbilt, and is still around today. In the same period the UK also saw a new wave of enthusiasm for the idea of socially motivated but commercially run enterprises thanks to Victorian housing reformers such as Octavia Hill, George Peabody and Edward Guinness, all of whom experimented with building affordable dwellings that were let to working class tenants at below-market rates as a form of 'percentage philanthropy'.[23]

The idea of combining profit and purpose is clearly not new, but it has been rediscovered by a wider audience recently thanks to the growth of approaches like microfinance and impact investing. These have the potential to offer innovative funding methods for tackling social and environmental problems, but many still harbour nagging doubts about them. As with previous attempts throughout history to blend financial and social motivations, critics worry that the profit motive will win out and end up shifting social finance approaches ever more towards pure commercialism.

There is also an unanswered question about how blended approaches relate to traditional philanthropy: do those making social investments see them as coming out of the same pot as their philanthropic giving? If so, the danger is that they are merely cannibalizing money that would otherwise be given out as gifts, not increasing the money going towards social good overall. If, however, the money used to make social investments is coming from the pot that would otherwise be used for profit-making, then perhaps these approaches are an invaluable way of growing the overall volume of resources available for good causes?

Making business more philanthropic

While many have put their efforts into trying to make philanthropy more businesslike, others argue that a far greater impact can be achieved by making business more philanthropic. The relative scale of money flows, they point out, is such that even a small shift towards greater social responsibility in the private sector is likely to have a much larger net effect than all but the most radical improvements in philanthropy. Of course, this needn't be either/or, and in practice efforts to improve business have often gone hand in hand with efforts to improve philanthropy. Opinion has sometimes been divided, however, on what the exact aim should be: is it enough for businesses simply to be more philanthropic in the sense of giving away money they have made to charitable organizations, or do we need to consider the wider social impact of the business and how its commercial operations need to change? There are obvious echoes here of the tainted money debate we explored in Chapter 3, as similar questions arise about whether we can separate how money is made from how it is subsequently used. As in the case of individual donors, recent years have seen greater demands to contextualize the philanthropy of companies against how they accumulated wealth in the first place. It may once have been possible for companies to present their corporate philanthropy in isolation, as a straightforward good (and sometimes as a fairly transparent PR exercise), but increasingly customers, employees and the public want to understand the wider picture, including the company's environmental impact, its tax affairs, how well it does on diversity, how fairly it treats its workers and so on.

The idea that businesses have social responsibilities is often presented as though it is dazzlingly modern, with a whole industry of glossy reports and buzzword-laden events now promoting concepts like 'purpose' and 'shared value'. But perhaps we have things the wrong way round. The idea that making money can be divorced from social responsibility may in fact be a relatively recent invention; since it would once have been taken as read that those in charge of companies had responsibilities to the wider society in which they live.

That was certainly true of the seventeenth-century London merchant Thomas Firmin, whose philanthropic approach to business led him to establish a number of 'projects for the imploying [*sic*] of the poor', which involved running deliberately loss-making textile companies with above-average wages and welfare conditions as a form of 'thrifty philanthropy'.[24] Firmin was an outlier, but the notion that business owners needed to demonstrate some sense of social responsibility seems to have been much more widely established. Often there was a degree of enlightened self-interest in employers' philanthropic efforts, so they would be first and foremost focused on their own employees. A notable example is the various model workers' towns and villages built by nineteenth-century industrialists such as George Cadbury (who built Bournville near Birmingham), William Lever (Port Sunlight on Merseyside) and Titus Salt (Saltaire in West Yorkshire). These provided homes for workers that were a huge improvement on the cramped and dirty urban dwellings of the time, but often came at the cost of paternalistic meddling in their lives (curfews, mandatory temperance and so on). And in an international context the same kind of enlightened self-interest combined with a colonial mindset to give rise to even more problematic examples of planned workers communities, such as Leverville in the Belgian Congo and Fordlandia in the Brazilian Amazon.

The Quakers perhaps took things furthest in terms of recognizing the social responsibilities of business. Their dissenting version of Protestantism regarded success in business as a key tool for demonstrating commitment to God, provided it was done according to the right principles. As a result, there were many prominent Quaker business leaders throughout the nineteenth century. Some were also high-profile philanthropists, such as confectionery manufacturers Joseph Rowntree and George Cadbury, both of whom had wide-ranging interests that constantly blurred the lines between philanthropy, business and politics. Indeed, it has been said of Cadbury that

> he was contemptuous of the rich men who devoted the morning and noon of their lives to making money and the evening to giving it away, and of those who kept their money-making and their benevolent activities in well-insulated compartments.[25]

Other groups who, like the Quakers, were marginalized from mainstream society have similarly shown a

Figure 6.2: Madam C.J. Walker. Photograph by Addison Spurlock, c. 1914

Madam C. J. Walker was a pioneering businesswoman and philanthropist in the early twentieth century. She created a hugely successful range of hair care and beauty products, which led her to become the first self-made female millionaire – a feat made even more remarkable by the fact she did it at a time of racial segregation, when opportunities for Black women were severely limited. She was a committed philanthropist throughout her life and used her personal wealth and her business in a wide range of innovative ways to support Black causes and the nascent civil rights movement.

willingness to blur the lines between business and philanthropy. As philanthropy scholar Tyrone McKinley Freeman notes, this was very much the case for Black Americans in the early twentieth century, as they 'did not have the luxury of thinking in a sector-based compartmentalized manner'. Instead, black philanthropists, including notable figures like the beauty care entrepreneur Madam C.J. Walker, had to 'work across the boundaries of markets, governments and social services' and use 'any available means of meeting their own needs and working for societal change'.[26]

In the twentieth century the financialization of business and the growth of models in which companies' first allegiance was now to increasingly powerful corporate shareholders meant that more and more investors questioned the idea that companies should be philanthropic or have social responsibilities. Perhaps most influential here were the arguments of economist Milton Friedman, who famously declared that 'the social responsibility of business is to increase its profits'.[27]

Friedman accepted that individuals who work in a company might have social responsibilities but claimed that within a corporate business, any actions taken to discharge that responsibility which reduced the return to shareholders, raised prices for customers or lowered employees' wages amounted to 'spending their money' rather than your own. Some wealthy business owners who dismiss the idea of wider corporate social responsibility have further argued they are doing enough good in society already through their commercial activities. John Paul Getty famously said that 'the best form of charity I know is the art of meeting a payroll',[28] words echoed years later by the Mexican billionaire Carlos Slim Helú when he said that he could 'do more good by building solid companies than by going around like Santa Claus donating money'.[29] More recently, there seems to be a clear belief among big figures in the tech industry that the products and platforms that have made them so rich are also the best way to solve the world's problems. Hence Elon Musk's declaration in an interview in 2022 that his commercial companies Tesla, SpaceX and Neuralink are 'all philanthropy' and a reflection of his overarching ambition to 'extend the light of consciousness to the stars'.[30]

Where now, where next?

Philanthropy and business are inextricably linked, but what this means in practice for both is not always clear. There are plenty who hold with the tenets of philanthrocapitalism and believe that the tools and approaches of the commercial world can be used to address what they see as the flaws of philanthropy. If all parties are on the same page, this can result in genuine innovation through models like 'venture philanthropy', where donors bring a blend of financial support and business experience to the table and work with charitable organizations in a highly engaged way to improve their efficiency and impact. Likewise, there is 'social investment', where donors use their resources to support recipient organizations in ways that combine social and financial return. If, however, business principles are put on a pedestal or their use becomes dogmatic, this can be damaging for all concerned. As we have seen, throughout history when communities have ideas imposed on them from above without taking into account their actual needs and wishes, it tends not to end well.

A famous example is that of PlayPumps. These are playground roundabouts that also function as water pumps, developed in the early 2000s to provide an innovative solution to the challenges faced by women and children in sub-Saharan Africa spending hours each day collecting water. Instead, it was claimed, children could simply play and pump water at the same time. However, over time it became clear that, despite being installed in thousands of towns and villages, in many cases the PlayPumps were ill-suited to local conditions and children saw them not as play but simply as more work, so they went unused. Funders such as the Case Foundation subsequently acknowledged that their enthusiasm for the neatness of PlayPumps as an apparent solution had blinded them to their flaws.[31]

At the same time, the context for businesses is evolving rapidly. Changing public attitudes mean there is growing expectation from consumers and employees that companies are not only financially successful but also able to demonstrate a positive social and environmental impact. Many companies have enthusiastically embraced this, putting wider social purpose at the core of what they do, rather than seeing it merely as an afterthought through a corporate philanthropy programme (as was often the case until recently). A growing number are even building social responsibility into the fabric of their organizations through adopting new models such as the 'B Corporation' (or B Corp), a globally recognized certification scheme for companies' social purpose. Notable B Corps so far include ice cream manufacturer Ben & Jerry's, food company Danone North America and outdoor clothing manufacturer Patagonia.

As the range of possibilities for people to do good or demonstrate a purpose grows, it raises a fundamental question: what is the value of philanthropy in this context? There is a risk that if we accept the blurring of boundaries between philanthropy and the market it will erode the distinctiveness of philanthropic approaches. But does this matter if the overall amount of good being done is the same or greater? Or is there a unique value to the idea of giving private money away to produce public good without any expectation of a financial return that is worth protecting? It may well be that there are good reasons to be cautious; in the same way that some companies have been accused of engaging in 'greenwashing' by using tree-planting programmes and other initiatives to deflect criticism of their wider environmental harms, there are signs that measures and markers of social responsibility such as the B Corporation certification have in some cases been used for 'purpose washing' by companies keen to bask in the halo effect of recognized social responsibility credentials to mask scrutiny of their operations, employment practices or tax affairs. In 2021, the B Corp status of brewing company BrewDog was put under review following a complaint from a former employee about its working practices.[32] Similarly in 2022, criticism of employment conditions at the Kenyan office of content moderation firm Sama led to calls for it to be stripped of B Corp status.[33] In neither case so far has action been taken, leading some to question whether lack of suitable enforcement mechanisms devalues the B Corp as a mark of genuine social purpose.

7
CONCLUSION: WHERE NEXT FOR PHILANTHROPY?

Finding an exact definition of philanthropy on which all can agree remains elusive, but our exploration of various alternatives has drawn out many distinguishing features, themes and questions that should at least allow us to tackle the question of what philanthropy is *for* with more confidence.

Philanthropy, we have seen, is not charity. Rather than focusing on dealing with the symptoms of problems at an individual level, philanthropy seeks to address their root causes at a systemic level. As a result, it needs to be led primarily by the head, rather than the heart, and to focus on using data and measurement to ensure that interventions are effective and efficient (difficult though this can be). Yet we have also seen that this can bring criticism if it leads philanthropists to impose technocratic, top-down approaches on the people and communities they are supposedly trying to help. In the worst cases, the pursuit of rationality and universality led some philanthropists in the past to lose sight of basic humanity and compassion, with deeply disturbing consequences that still cast a long shadow over philanthropy. A growing number of donors and funders now recognize these dangers and acknowledge the need for a balance between the systematic, strategic approaches that have typified philanthropy and the human-centred approaches that have too often been derided as 'mere charity'.

Philanthropy, we are also told, is not justice. Charity is a choice on the part of the donor to give a gift, which the recipient is expected to be grateful for, but cannot expect. Justice, on the other hand, places a duty on the giver to make a payment, which the recipient can demand as a matter of rights, and need not show gratitude for. It is important that we are clear about this distinction and do not try to make philanthropy an inadequate substitute for justice. Yet at the same time, we can still have the ambition to make philanthropy a more effective (if never perfect) tool for furthering justice, by changing the ways in which it is done. We can, for instance, minimize intergenerational injustice by questioning norms of perpetuity for endowments. A growing number of new donors are doing this and making their approaches time-limited from the outset, while organizations such as the Edward W. Hazen Foundation are choosing to move away from permanence and instead to spend down their endowments over coming years. We can also ensure that philanthropy is not a force for perpetuating injustices committed in the creation of wealth by addressing the challenges posed by tainted donations and contextualizing where money has come from. A number of UK charitable foundations, including the John Ellerman Foundation, the Joseph Rowntree Foundation and the Joseph Rowntree Charitable Trust, are all doing work to better understand potentially problematic elements of their own histories and how to grapple with them. In some cases, greater transparency around sources of wealth may be enough; in others it may need to pave the way for further action in the form of reparations or measures designed to address past injustices.

Philanthropists can also choose to support social movements and grassroots organizations seeking to change the very systems and structures that they as donors may have benefitted from. This may be challenging for donors, as demonstrated by the example of FRIDA, the young feminist fund, which accepted a $10 million donation from Mackenzie Scott while at the same time issuing a statement that condemned the source of Scott's wealth (Amazon).[1] It may also be challenging for the recipient organizations if they find that well-meaning but risk-averse donors try to attach strings to their support which constrain the ability to speak out or to engage in certain activities. The risk of 'movement capture' remains very real, as evidenced by concerns that foundations which have proclaimed their support for the Black Lives Matter movement are trying to steer the conversation away from some of the movement's more radical demands towards a less confrontational 'reform' agenda.[2]

Philanthropy must also be understood in contrast to the state. Both have strengths and weaknesses: philanthropy can be agile and innovative, but is shaped by the preferences of individuals and thus not good at guaranteeing fairness and equity. The state, meanwhile, can offer universality and consistency, but is sometimes inflexible and risk-averse. It is clear, however, that philanthropy should not be seen as an alternative to public spending because of the mismatch in both scale and distribution. Philanthropy must therefore be clearer about the roles it can play in relation to the state. This might be working in partnership with public sector bodies to deliver services that are more person-centred or grounded in communities; it might be pioneering and testing new approaches that the state is subsequently able to adopt; or it might be challenging state provision through advocacy and campaigning designed to make provision better in the future. All of these are vital functions that philanthropy can play, but we must be clearer as a society about what we expect the state to provide and what we are happy for philanthropy to do.

Philanthropy, we have seen, is not a substitute for taxation either. The two serve different social functions, so philanthropy should never be an excuse for avoiding paying a fair share of tax. In fact, some would argue that it is the responsibility of any philanthropist concerned about inequality and injustice to argue for *higher* taxes on wealth in addition their giving, as groups such as Patriotic Millionaires are doing. We should also question the tax treatment of philanthropy itself: instead of taking tax relief on charitable donations for granted, we should ask what, if anything, is the appropriate rationale for governments offering such incentives? If, as this book has argued, they only make sense when understood as a generalized subsidy for individual support of a healthy, pluralistic civil society, then what are the implications for how they should be structured and how generous they should be?

We have seen that philanthropy has the potential to act as an anti-democratic force. It can introduce a plutocratic bias towards the interests of the wealthy or allow the 'dead hand of the donor' to exert undue influence through perpetual endowments. On the other hand, we have seen that it can also strengthen democracy, playing a vital role in ensuring we have a pluralistic civil society that allows marginalized voices to be heard and providing as a counterbalance to the tyranny of the majority. It can also act as a 'nursery of democracy' which fosters civic engagement and teaches skills of democratic participation. It is vital that philanthropy acknowledges this dual nature, and that we understand what can be done to ensure that it plays a positive role in democratic societies in the future.

We can minimize the risk of plutocratic bias by demanding greater transparency and openness within philanthropy and by ensuring that philanthropic funders look to fund civil society organizations and social movements that are able to call upon a wider base of support, so that their own money does not have a disproportionate effect. We must be careful, however, that in doing so we do not undermine philanthropy's ability to challenge the status quo and support unpopular or marginalized causes, because it is precisely this ability that has allowed philanthropy to play such a vital role throughout history in bringing issues from the margins to the mainstream and driving long-term social change. A key part of maintaining this ability will be protecting the rights and freedoms that organizations and social movements need in order to speak truth to power, so philanthropy must join efforts to defend civil society against regressive policies and laws around the world.

It is also important that philanthropy recognizes the responsibility to play a role in driving discovery and innovation. This doesn't mean that all funders have to be constantly chasing new things – sometimes nurturing or protecting what we already have is innovative in itself – but it does mean that philanthropists must look for opportunities to take risks that the state or the market cannot, in order to push forward on social and environmental issues. At the same time, we must ask whether philanthropy itself needs to be more democratic if it is to maximize its potential. Are the philanthropic organizations and institutions we currently have reflective of society as a whole and of the people and communities they are trying to serve? If not, then we need to make more concerted efforts to ensure greater diversity and representation. This may simply be through re-examining the make-up of the workforce in philanthropic organizations, or through adopting participatory models which bring the people and communities that would traditionally have been seen as the passive beneficiaries of philanthropy into more active decision-making roles. We also need to ensure that the practicalities of how philanthropic funding is given out allow power, as well as financial resources, to be shifted: this means moving away from norms of short-term, donor-directed and restricted funding and instead embracing longer-term, trust-based models in which recipient organizations are given support for their core costs and afforded freedom to decide how money is spent.

Finally, we must acknowledge that philanthropy is not the market. While there are certainly skills and insights from the commercial world that philanthropic organizations and donors can draw on, we should not put these on a pedestal or assume they automatically apply in the context of complex and often deeply entrenched social and environmental problems. We should welcome the growing number of businesses which put social purpose at the heart of their own operations, and philanthropists and civil society organizations should look to understand how they can work in partnership with purpose-led companies. However, as this trend becomes widespread, we must also guard against the risk that the concept of 'social purpose' gets so diluted as to become meaningless, or that unscrupulous companies engage in 'purpose washing' by adopting the language and markers of social purpose without changing how they operate. More fundamentally, as market-based approaches to social issues grow in popularity and prominence, we must have far greater clarity about what, if anything, is the remaining unique value of philanthropy and dedicated nonprofit organizations.

An ideal version of philanthropy?

This book has attempted to outline the key questions we need to be asking in order to understand what philanthropy is for, and how we can go about doing it in a way that ensures it acts as a positive force within society. Of course, it is likely that we will all come up with different answers to these questions, and that any notion of an ideal form of philanthropy will remain in the eye of the beholder. But perhaps this does not matter. In fact, maybe it is healthy, because philanthropy is fundamentally based on choices and decisions made by individuals so it *should* be as diverse and varied as those individuals themselves. What does matter is that we all have a shared understanding of the choices that have been made and why, and that we are able to accept these choices or to challenge them in a constructive way when needed. Too often debates about philanthropy collapse into polarized polemic that breeds only defensiveness and resentment and moves nothing forward. We need instead to able to deal with nuance and complexity: to answer criticism in some cases, or to accept it in others and use it to improve philanthropy so it can become the best version of itself. That way, we will all benefit.

NOTES

Chapter 1

1   Charities Aid Foundation (CAF), *UK Giving 2021*.

2   A. Pruitt, and J. Bergdoll, 'Americans gave a record $471 billion to charity in 2020, amid concerns about the coronavirus pandemic, job losses and racial justice', *The Conversation*, 15 June 2022.

3   P.D. Johnson et al, *Global Philanthropy Report: Perspectives on the Global Foundation Sector* (Hauser Institute for Civil Society at the John F. Kennedy School of Government, Harvard University, 2018).

4   OECD, *Private Philanthropy for Development – Second Edition: Data for Action* (OECD Publishing, 2021).

5   Data taken from Wikipedia, 'List of wealthiest charitable foundations'. Dollar values calculated using exchange rates correct as of 31 December 2020. It is worth noting that reliance on data gathered via Wikipedia is far from ideal; however, there are few other sources of comparative data on global foundation assets and those that do exist have significant methodological flaws which make them no more reliable than this list. This reflects the broader point that data on foundations is frustratingly hard to come by, due to wide variations in transparency requirements and reporting timescales around the globe, as well as definitional issues around what should count as a philanthropic foundation.

6   Data taken from Johnson et al, *Global Philanthropy Report*.

7   D.F. Burlinghame, 'Altruism and Philanthropy: definitional issues', *Essays on Philanthropy: no. 10*, (Indiana University Center on Philanthropy, 1993), p. 6.

8   R. Payton and M. Moody, *Understanding Philanthropy: Its Meaning and Mission* (Indiana University Press, 2008).

Chapter 2

1   *Pembroke County Guardian and Cardigan Reporter*, 27 July 1905, p. 9.

2   Charities Aid Foundation, *UK Giving 2021* and the Giving Institute, *Giving USA 2021*.

3   W.K. Jordan, *Philanthropy in England 1480–1660* (George Allen & Unwin, 1959), pp. 18–19.

4   Sermon no. 10: Preached at Lincoln's Inn, in Simpson and Potter (eds.), *The Sermons of John Donne* (University of California Press, 1953).

5   G. Jones, *History of the Law of Charity 1532–1827* (Cambridge University Press, 1969), p. 10.

6   'Of goodness and goodness of nature' in F. Bacon, *Essays* (W.L. Allison, 1888).

7   H. Cunningham, *The Reputation of Philanthropy Since 1750: Britain and Beyond* (Manchester University Press, 2020).

8   D. Owen, *English Philanthropy: 1660–1960* (Harvard University Press, 1965), p. 92.

9   R.A. Gross, 'Giving in America: from charity to philanthropy', in Friedman and McGarvie (eds.), *Charity, Philanthropy, and Civility in American History* (Cambridge University Press, 2002), pp. 29–48.

10   Cited in B. Soskis, *Both More and No More: The Historical Split between Charity and Philanthropy* (Hudson Institute, 2014), p. 15.

11   W.S. Gilbert, *The Bab Ballads, with Which are Included Songs of a Savoyard* (Macmillan, 1904).

12   'On Doing Good', *The Times*, 12 May 1914, p. 9.

13   J. Swift, *A Modest Proposal and Other Writings* (Penguin UK, 2009).

14   G. Cruikshank, 'The Universal Philanthropist', in H. Mayhew (ed.) *The Comic Almanack, for 1848: Illustrated by George Cruikshank* (Vizetelly Brothers and Co., 1848).

15   J. Tenniel, 'Telescopic Philanthropy', *Punch*, 4 March 1865.

16   G. Canning, C. Edmonds and J. Gillray, *Poetry of the Anti-Jacobin: Comprising the Celebrated Political & Satirical Poems, Parodies, and Jeux-d'esprit of the Rt Hon. George Canning and Others* (Willis, 1852), p. 201.

17   'Ode to Modern Philanthropy', *The Times*, 28 December 1840.

18   J. Tremblay-Boire, A. Prakash and M.A. Calderon, 'Delivering Public Services to the Underserved: Nonprofits and the Latino Threat Narrative', *Public Administration Review* (2022).

19   A. Carnegie, 'The Gospel of Wealth', *The North American Review*, 183(599), (1906), pp. 526–37, p. 535.

20   Taken from the account of 15 April 1778 in J. Boswell (Wallace ed.), *The Life of Samuel Johnson, LL. D.* (W.P. Nimmo, 1873), p. 377.

21 W.S. Jevons, *Political Economy* (D. Appleton & Co., 1880), p. 9.

22 P. Slack, *The English Poor Law, 1531–1782* (Cambridge University Press, 1995), p. 41.

23 M. Lindemann, *Patriots and Paupers: Hamburg, 1712–1830* (Oxford University Press, 1990), p. 147.

24 Owen, *English Philanthropy*, p. 92.

25 This is a quote widely attributed to Carnegie and often claimed to come from 'The Gospel of Wealth'; however there is no evidence of it in any versions of that article. The closest paraphrase the author has been able to find appears in a letter from Carnegie to US President Theodore Roosevelt dated 28 January 1908, in which Carnegie writes 'you have a hard task at present but the distribution of money judiciously is not without its difficulties and involves harder work than ever acquisition of wealth did'. T. Roosevelt (1907) Theodore Roosevelt Papers: Series 1: Letters and Related Material,1759–1919; 1907, Dec. 13–1908, Feb. 14. [Manuscript/Mixed Material] Retrieved from the Library of Congress, https://www.loc.gov/item/mss382990080/. Images 595 & 596.

26 J.B. O'Reilly, 'In Bohemia' (1886), reprinted in Sinclair (ed.), *The Cry for Justice: An Anthology of the Literature of Social Protest* (Upton Sinclair, 1915), p. 497.

27 'Charity', in A. Bierce, *The Shadow on the Dial, And Other Essays* (A.M. Robertson, 1909), p. 175.

28 J. Addams, 'Charitable Effort' (1902), reprinted in O'Connell (ed.) *America's Voluntary Spirit: A Book of Readings* (The Foundation Center, 1983), pp. 73–80, p. 75.

29 W. Bagehot, *Physics and Politics, or Thoughts on the Application of the Principles of 'Natural Selection' and 'Inheritance' to Political Theory* (Henry S. King, 1872), p. 189.

30 C. Darwin, *The Descent of Man, and Selection in Relation to Sex* (John Murray Press, 1896), p. 134.

31 A. Rutherford, *Control: The Dark History and Troubling Present of Eugenics* (Orion, 2021).

32 H.S. Jennings, 'Biological Aspects of Charity', in Faris, Laune and Todd (eds.) *Intelligent Philanthropy* (1930, reprinted Patterson Smith, 1960), p. 271.

33 W.A. Schambra, 'Philanthropy's Original Sin', *The New Atlantis* (October 2013), pp. 3–21.

34 J. Butler, *Woman's Work and Woman's Culture* (Macmillan and Co., 1869), p. xxxvii.

35   P. Singer, *The Most Good You Can Do* (Yale University Press, 2015).

36   N. Kenworthy et al, 'A cross-sectional study of social inequities in medical crowdfunding campaigns in the United States', *PLoS ONE*, 15(3): e0229760, (2020).

Chapter 3

1   Quoted in P.D. Hall, 'Philanthropy, the nonprofit sector & the democratic dilemma', *Daedalus*, 142(2), (2013), pp. 139–58.

2   Quoted in G.B. Finlayson, *Citizen, State, and Social Welfare in Britain 1830–1990* (Oxford University Press, 1994), p. 249.

3   B. Russell, 'On Charity', *New York American*, 2 November 1932. Reproduced in Russell, *Mortals and Others* (Routledge Classics, 2009), pp. 129–30.

4   M. Ryan, '"To mistake gold for wealth": The Venerable Bede and the fate of Northumbria', in Cooper and Leyser (eds.), *Making Early Medieval Societies: Conflict and Belonging in the Latin West, 300–1200* (Cambridge University Press, 2016), pp. 80–103.

5   D. Owen, *English Philanthropy: 1660–1690* (Harvard University Press, 1965), p. 437.

6   E. Saunders-Hastings, '"Send back the bloodstained money": Frederick Douglass on tainted gifts', *American Political Science Review*, 115(3), (2021), pp. 729–41.

7   G.B. Shaw, 'Preface to Major Barbara: first aid to critics', in *Major Barbara* (Brentano's, 1907), p. 23.

8   T. Roosevelt, Address of President Roosevelt at the laying of the corner stone of the office building of the House of Representatives (also known as 'The Man with the Muckrake'), 14 April 1906. Reproduced by Voices of Democracy: The US Oratory Project.

9   'A humane word from Satan', *Harper's Weekly*, 8 April 1905. Reproduced in M. Twain, *The $30,000 Dollar Bequest and Other Stories* (Harper & Brothers, 1906), pp. 237–9.

10   G.K. Chesterton, 'Gifts of the millionaire', *Illustrated London News*, 29 May 1909.

11   A. Hern, 'Charities in a bind after cybercriminals donate $10,000 in bitcoin', *Guardian*, 20 October 2020.

12   J.B. Schneewind, 'Philosophical ideas of charity: some historical reflections', in Schneewind (ed.) *Giving: Western Ideas of Philanthropy* (Indiana University Press, 1996), pp. 54–75, p. 55.

13   Thomas Aquinas, *Summa Theologica*, Part II-II, Question 66: 'Of theft and robbery'.

14 J.B. Schneewind, 'Philosophical ideas of charity: some historical reflections'.

15 S. Forde, 'The Charitable John Locke', *Review of Politics* 71(3), (2009), pp. 428–58.

16 J.B. Schneewind, 'Philosophical ideas of charity: some historical reflections'.

17 M. Wollstonecraft, *A Vindication of the Rights of Men, in a letter to the Right Honourable Edmund Burke; occasioned by his Reflections on the Revolution in France* (J. Johnson, 1790), p. 133.

18 W. Godwin, *An Enquiry Concerning Political Justice: and its Influence on General Virtue and Happiness*, Vol II (G.G.J. and J. Robinson, 1793), p. 798.

19 T. Paine, *Agrarian Justice, Opposed to Agrarian Law, and to Agrarian Monopoly* (W. Adlard, 1797).

20 I. Kant (Infield ed.), *Lectures on Ethics* (Methuen & Co, 1930), p. 194.

21 E. Durkheim and H. Joas, 'General Duties of Social Life. (2) Charity' in Gross and Jones (eds.), *Durkheim's Philosophy Lectures: Notes from the Lycée de Sens Course, 1883–1884* (Cambridge University Press, 2004), pp. 270–71.

22 E. Zola (trans. E.A. Vizetelly), *Paris* (Macmillan, 1898), p. 730.

23 F. Engels (trans. F.K. Wischnewetzy), *The Condition of the Working Class in England: From Personal Observation and Authentic Sources* (George Allen and Unwin, 1892; reprinted 1952), p. 278.

24 O. Wilde, *The Soul of Man Under Socialism and Selected Critical Prose* (Arthur L. Humphreys, 1912), p. 10.

25 M.L. King, *Strength to Love* (Harper & Row, 1963; reprinted Fortress Press, 1981), p. 34.

26 L. Hughes, 'To Negro writers'. Reproduced in L. Hughes et al. *The Collected Works of Langston Hughes: Essays on Art, Race, Politics, and World Affairs. Vol. 9* (University of Missouri Press, 2001), p. 132.

27 A. Andrews, 'Constructing mutuality: The Zapatistas' transformation of transnational activist power dynamics', *Latin American Politics and Society*, 52(1), (2010), pp. 89–120.

28 C. Cordelli, 'Reparative justice and the moral limits of discretionary philanthropy' in Reich, Cordelli and Bernholz (eds.), *Philanthropy in Democratic Societies* (University of Chicago Press, 2016), pp. 244–67, p. 247.

29 E. Villanueva, *Decolonizing Wealth: Indigenous Wisdom to Heal Divides and Restore Balance* (Berrett-Koehler Publishers, 2021).

30   Millionaires for Humanity sign-on letter, July 2020. https://
     millionairesforhumanity.org/sign-on-letter/
31   D. Owen, *English Philanthropy: 1660–1690*, p. 132.
32   J.M. Johnson, *Funding Feminism: Monied Women, Philanthropy
     and the Women's Movement 1870–1967* (The University of North
     Carolina Press, 2017), p. 2.
33   M.M. Francis, 'The price of civil rights: Black lives, white funding,
     and movement capture', *Law & Society Review*, 53(1), (2019),
     pp. 275–309.
34   K. Ferguson, *Top Down: The Ford Foundation, Black Power,
     and the Reinvention of Racial Liberalism* (University of
     Pennsylvania Press, 2013); A. O'Connor, 'The Ford Foundation
     and philanthropic activism in the 1960s', in Lagemann (ed.),
     Philanthropic Foundations: New Scholarship, New Possibilities
     (Indiana University Press, 1999), pp. 169–94.

Chapter 4

1   A.P. Chekhov, letter to A.F. Koni, 16 January 1891, in *Letters of
     Anton Chekhov to His Family and Friends* (trans. C.B. Garnett,
     The MacMillan Company, 1920), p. 228.
2   B.K. Gray, *Philanthropy and the State: or Social Politics* (P.S. King
     & Son, 1908), p. 3.
3   J.J. Fishman, 'Regulating the Poor and Encouraging Charity in
     Times of Crisis: The Poor Laws and the Statute of Charitable Uses',
     Pace Law Faculty Publications, 406, (2007).
4   W.K. Jordan, *Philanthropy in England 1480–1660* (George Allen
     & Unwin, 1959), p. 75.
5   B.K. Gray, *A History of English Philanthropy: From the
     Dissolution of the Monasteries to the Taking of the First Census*,
     p. 285.
6   Charitable Trusts Committee (Nathan Committee), *Report of the
     Committee on the Law and Practice Relating to Charitable Trusts*
     (Stationery Office, 1952), p. 8.
7   P. Thane, 'There has always been a "big society"', History
     Workshop blog, 30 April 2011. https://www.historyworkshop.org.
     uk/there-has-always-been-a-big-society/
8   'Charitable London', *The Times*, 7 September 1850, p. 6.
9   Quoted in G.B. Finlayson, *Citizen, State, and Social Welfare in
     Britain 1830–1990* (Oxford University Press, 1994), p. 272.
10   Hansard, *H.C. Deb., vol. 422, cc. 43–142, 30 April 1946.*

11   Charitable Trusts Committee (Nathan Committee), *Report of the Committee on the Law and Practice Relating to Charitable Trusts*, p. 160.

12   Quoted in G.B. Finlayson, *Citizen, State, and Social Welfare in Britain 1830–1990*, p. 281.

13   Detroit Historical Society, *Encyclopedia of Detroit: Grand Bargain*.

14   B.K. Gray, *Philanthropy and the State: or Social Politics*, p. 4.

15   J.L. Riley, 'Was the $5 billion worth it?', *Washington Post*, 23 July 2011.

16   P. Sullivan, 'Private citizen Bloomberg on philanthropy', *New York Times,* 25 April 2014.

17   W. Beveridge, *Voluntary Action: A Report on Methods of Social Advance* (George Allen & Unwin, 1948), p. 302.

18   Hansard, *H.C. Deb. vol. 155, cc. 1198–221, 20 June 1922.*

19   R. Reich, 'Toward a political theory of philanthropy', in Illingworth, Pogge and Wenar (eds.) *Giving Well: The Ethics of Philanthropy* (Oxford University Press, 2011), pp. 177–95.

20   Hansard, *H.C. Deb., vol. 170, cc. 1067–136, 4 May 1863.*

21   Quoted in M.J. Gousmett, 'The Charitable Purposes Exemption from Income Tax: Pitt to Pemsel 1798–1891', Unpublished PhD Thesis (University of Canterbury, New Zealand, 2009), p. 514.

22   OECD, *Taxation and Philanthropy*, OECD Tax Policy Studies, no. 27 (OECD Publishing, 2020).

23   J. Andreoni, and J. Durnford, 'Effects of the TCJA on itemization status and charitable deduction', *Tax Notes Federal*, 26 August 2019.

Chapter 5

1   Quoted in P.D. Hall, 'Philanthropy, the nonprofit sector & the democratic dilemma', *Daedalus*, 142(2), (2013), pp. 139–58.

2   Charitable Trusts Committee (Nathan Committee), *Report of the Committee on the Law and Practice Relating to Charitable Trusts* (Stationery Office, 1952), p. 12.

3   F.P. Walsh, 'Perilous Philanthropy', *Independent*, 83, pp. 262–64.

4   R. Reich, *Just Giving: Why Philanthropy is Failing Democracy and How It Can Do Better* (Princeton University Press, 2018), pp. 7–8.

5   Quoted in J.A. Clarke, 'Turgot's critique of perpetual endowments', *French Historical Studies* 3(4), (1964), pp. 495–506.

6   J.S. Mill, 'Endowments', *Fortnightly Review* 5(28), (1869), pp. 377–90.

7   A. Hobhouse, *The Dead Hand: Addresses on the Subject of Endowments and Settlements of Property* (Spottiswoode & Co., 1880), p. 44.

8   D. Owen, 'The City parochial charities: the "dead hand" in late Victorian London', *Journal of British Studies*, 1(2), (1962), pp. 115–35.

9   'Limiting the Foundation', *Springfield Republican*, 9 March 1910.

10   J. Rosenwald, 'Principles of Public Giving', (1929). Reproduced in Kass (ed.), *Giving Well, Doing Good: Readings for Thoughtful Philanthropists* (Indiana University Press, 2008), pp. 185–93.

11   Quoted in E. Brayer, *George Eastman: A Biography* (University of Rochester Press, 2006), p. 346.

12   W.K. Jordan, *Philanthropy in England 1480–1660* (George Allen & Unwin, 1959), p. 149.

13   F.K. Prochaska, 'Philanthropy', in Thompson (ed.) *The Cambridge Social History of Britain 1750–1950 (3): Social Agencies and Institutions* (Cambridge University Press, 1990), p. 370.

14   Quoted in K. Waddington, *Charity and the London Hospitals, 1850–1898* (Boydell & Brewer Ltd, 2000), pp. 30–1.

15   B. Whitaker, *The Foundations: An Anatomy of Philanthropy and Society* (Eyre Methuen, 1974), p. 53.

16   Quoted in R. Magat, *Unlikely Partners: Philanthropic Foundations and the Labor Movement* (Cornell University Press, 1999), p. 90.

17   Quoted in G.B. Finlayson, *Citizen, State, and Social Welfare in Britain 1830–1990* (Oxford University Press, 1994), p. 130.

18   D. Walker, 'Toward a new gospel of wealth', Ford Foundation blog, 1 October 2015. https://www.fordfoundation.org/news-and-stories/stories/posts/toward-a-new-gospel-of-wealth/

19   M.M. Francis and E. Kohl-Arenas, 'Here we go again: philanthropy & movement capture', *The Forge*, 17 June 2021.

20   R.J. Morris, 'Clubs, societies and associations', in Thompson (ed.), *The Cambridge Social History of Britain 1750–1950(3): Social Agencies and Institutions* (Cambridge University Press, 1990), pp. 395–444, p. 436.

21   Quoted in P.D. Hall, 'A historical overview of philanthropy, voluntary associations and nonprofit organizations in the United States 1600–2000', in Powell and Steinberg (eds.) *The Nonprofit Sector: A Research Handbook* (second edition, Yale University Press, 2006), pp. 32–65, p. 35.

22   Quoted in P. D. Hall, 'Resolving the Dilemmas of Democratic Governance. The Historical Development of Trusteeship in

America', in E.C. Lagemann (ed.), *Philanthropic Foundations: New Scholarship, New Possibilities* (Indiana University Press, 1999), pp. 3–42, p. 9.

23 J.S. Mill, 'Endowments', *Fortnightly Review* 5(28), (1869), pp. 377–90.

24 Quoted in D. Owen, *English Philanthropy: 1660–1960* (Harvard University Press, 1965), p. 327.

25 F.A. Hayek and R. Hamowy (eds.) *The Constitution of Liberty: The Definitive Edition* (University of Chicago Press, 2011), p. 192.

26 D. Callahan, *The Givers: Wealth, Power, and Philanthropy in a New Gilded Age* (Vintage, 2017), p. 166.

27 B.I. Page, L.M. Bartels and J. Seawright, 'Democracy and the policy preferences of wealthy Americans', *Perspectives on Politics*, 11(1), (2013), pp. 51–73.

28 W. Weaver, *U.S. Philanthropic Foundations: Their History, Structure, Management and Record* (Harper & Row, 1967), p. 200.

29 R. Reich, *Just Giving: Why Philanthropy is Failing Democracy and How It Can Do Better*, p. 159.

30 M. Mazzucato, *The Entrepreneurial State: Debunking Public vs. Private Sector Myths* (Anthem Press, 2013).

31 R. Lane, 'Bill Gates gets why people are doubting billionaires – and he has a defense (even for Mark Zuckerberg)', *Forbes*, 19 February 2019.

32 Charitable Trusts Committee (Nathan Committee), *Report of the Committee on the Law and Practice Relating to Charitable Trusts* (Stationery Office, 1952), p. 14.

33 D. Owen, *English Philanthropy: 1660–1690* (Harvard University Press, 1965), p. 474.

34 R. Reich, *Just Giving: Why Philanthropy is Failing Democracy and How It Can Do Better*, p. 166.

35 R.D. Putnam, R. Leonardi and R. Nanetti, *Making Democracy Work: Civic Traditions in Modern Italy* (Princeton University Press, 1993), p. 90.

36 F.K. Prochaska, *Schools of Citizenship: Charity and Civic Virtue* (Civitas/Institute for the Study of Civil Society, 2002), p. 14.

37 J.D. Smith and M. Oppenheimer, 'The Labour Movement and Voluntary Action in the UK and Australia: A comparative perspective', *Labour History* 88, (2005), pp. 105–20.

38 C. Braithwaite, *The Voluntary Citizen: An Enquiry into the Place of Philanthropy in the Community* (Methuen, 1938), p. 80.

39   F.K. Prochaska, *Women and Philanthropy in Nineteenth-Century England* (Oxford University Press, 1980), p. 227.
40   F.K. Prochaska, *Women and Philanthropy in Nineteenth-Century England*, p. 2.
41   K.D. McCarthy, 'Parallel power structures: Women and the voluntary sphere', in D. Hammack (ed.), *Making the Nonprofit Sector in the United States: A Reader* (Indiana University Press, 1998), pp. 248–63, p. 263.
42   R.J. Morris, 'Voluntary societies and British urban elites, 1780–1850: An analysis', *The Historical Journal*, 26(1), (1983), pp. 95–118, p. 115.
43   B. Harrison, 'Civil society by accident? Paradoxes of voluntarism and pluralism in the nineteenth and twentieth centuries', in Harris (ed.) *Civil Society in British History: Ideas, Identities, Institutions* (Oxford University Press, 2003), pp. 79–96, p. 95.
44   J. Roelofs, *Foundations and Public Policy: The Mask of Pluralism* (SUNY Press, 2003), p. 48.

Chapter 6

1   Smith and Cannan (eds.) *An Inquiry into the Nature and Causes of the Wealth of Nations* (The Modern Library, 1937), p. 14.
2   M. Bishop and M.F. Green, *Philanthrocapitalism: How the Rich Can Save the World, and Why We Should Let Them* (Bloomsbury, 2008).
3   W. Rathbone, *Social Duties: Considered with Reference to the Organization of Effort in Works of Benevolence and Public Utility* (Macmillan, 1867), pp. 65–6.
4   P. Shapely, *Charity and Power in Victorian Manchester* (Chetham Society, 2000), p. 29.
5   Quoted in P.D. Hall, 'Resolving the dilemmas of democratic governance: The historical development of trusteeship in America, 1636–1996', in Lagemann (ed.), *Philanthropic Foundations: New Scholarship, New Possibilities* (Indiana University Press, 1999), pp. 3–42, p. 26.
6   P.K. Angell, 'Julius Rosenwald', *The American Jewish Year Book*, 34, (1934), pp. 141–76.
7   M. Edwards, *Just Another Emperor: The Myths and Realities of Philanthrocapitalism* (Demos & The Young Foundation, 2008), p. 7.
8   P. Buchanan, 'The attack on philanthropy', Center for Strategic Philanthropy & Civil Society, Duke University, 10 November 2009.

9   D. Owen, *English Philanthropy: 1660–1960* (Harvard University Press, 1965), p. 57.

10 M.C. Samples, 'The humbug and the nightingale: P.T. Barnum, Jenny Lind, and the branding of a star singer for American reception' *The Musical Quarterly*, 99(3–4), (2017), pp. 286–320.

11 D. Owen, *English Philanthropy: 1660–1960* (Harvard University Press, 1965), p. 130.

12 F.K. Prochaska, *Women and Philanthropy in Nineteenth-Century England* (Oxford University Press, 1980).

13 S. Roddy, J.M. Strange and B. Taithe, *The Charity Market and Humanitarianism in Britain, 1870–1912* (Bloomsbury Publishing, 2020), p. 43.

14 'We publish this morning a list of charitable appeals...', *The Times*, 1 July 1880.

15 'Dancing Philanthropy', *North-Eastern Daily Gazette*, 31 May 1892.

16 E.H. Bayley, 'Nationalising the lifeboat service', *Westminster Review, Jan. 1852–Jan. 1914*, 147(2), (1897), pp. 120–27.

17 B. Harrison, 'Philanthropy and the Victorians', *Victorian Studies* 9(4), (1966), pp. 353–74.

18 A. Hands, *Charities and Social Aid in Greece and Rome* (Cornell University Press, 1968), pp. 109–10 and p. 184.

19 P. Vallely, *Philanthropy: From Aristotle to Zuckerberg* (Bloomsbury, 2020).

20 E. Chance et al, 'Charities for the poor', in Crossley and Elrington (eds.), *A History of the County of Oxford: Volume 4, the City of Oxford* (Victoria County History, 1979), pp. 462–75.

21 P. Brealey, 'The Charitable Corporation for the Relief of Industrious Poor: Philanthropy, Profit and Sleaze in London, 1707–1733', *History*, 98(333), (2013), pp. 708–29.

22 P. Vallely, *Philanthropy: From Aristotle to Zuckerberg*, p. 53.

23 D. Owen, *English Philanthropy: 1660–1960* (Harvard University Press, 1965), pp. 372–93.

24 D. Owen, *English Philanthropy: 1660–1960*, p. 18.

25 D. Owen, *English Philanthropy: 1660–1960*, pp. 434–35.

26 T.M. Freeman, *Madam C.J. Walker's Gospel of Giving: Black Women's Philanthropy during Jim Crow* (University of Illinois Press, 2020), p. 57.

27 M. Friedman, 'The social responsibility of business is to increase its profits', *New York Times*, 13 September 1970.

28   R. Miller, *The House of Getty* (Henry Holt and Company, 1986), p. 221.

29   A. Serrano, 'Billionaire pokes fun at philanthropy', *CBS Moneywatch*, 13 March 2007.

30   TED, 'Elon Musk: A future worth getting excited about', April 2022. https://www.ted.com/talks/elon_musk_a_future_worth_getting_excited_about?language=en

31   J. Case, 'The painful acknowledgment of coming up short', *Case Foundation*, 4 May 2010. https://casefoundation.org/blog/painful-acknowledgment-coming-short/

32   L. Clarence-Smith, 'BrewDog's ethical status at risk over allegations of "rotten culture"', *The Times*, 12 June 2021.

33   C. Mills Rodrigo, 'Corporate responsibility group reviewing Facebook contractor's worker treatment', *The Hill*, 11 May 2022.

Chapter 7

1   D. Ranganathan, 'Money is political', *Frida – The Young Feminist Fund* (2022). https://youngfeministfund.org/money-is-political/

2   M.M. Francis and E. Kohl-Arenas, 'Movement capture and the long arc of the Black freedom struggle', *HistPhil*, 14 July 2020.

FURTHER READING

Philanthropy or Charity?

Lucy Bernholz, *How We Give Now: A Philanthropic Guide for the Rest of Us* (MIT Press, 2021)

Robert Bremner, *Giving: Charity and Philanthropy in History* (Transaction Publishers, 1996)

Rhodri Davies, *Public Good by Private Means: How Philanthropy Shapes Britain* (Alliance Publishing Trust, 2016)

Lawrence Friedman and Mark McGarvie (eds.), *Charity, Philanthropy, and Civility in American History* (Cambridge University Press, 2003)

Peter Dobkin Hall, *Inventing the Nonprofit Sector and Other Essays on Philanthropy, Voluntarism, and Nonprofit Organizations* (Johns Hopkins University Press, 1992)

Warren Ilchman, Stanley Katz and Edward Queen (eds.), *Philanthropy in the World's Traditions* (Indiana University Press, 1998)

Wilbur K. Jordan, *Philanthropy in England, 1480–1660.* (George Allen and Unwin, 1959)

Michael Moody and Beth Breeze (eds.), *The Philanthropy Reader* (Routledge, 2016)

David Owen, *English Philanthropy, 1660–1960* (Harvard University Press, 1965)

Margaret Simey, *Charity Rediscovered: A Study of Philanthropic Effort in Nineteenth-Century Liverpool* (Liverpool University Press, 1992)

Benjamin Soskis, *Both More and No More: The historical split between charity and philanthropy* (Hudson Institute, 2014)

Paul Vallely, *Philanthropy: From Aristotle to Zuckerberg* (Bloomsbury Continuum, 2020)

Ben Whitaker, *The Foundations: An Anatomy of Philanthropy and Society* (Eyre Methuen, 1974)

Philanthropy or Justice?

Daniel Faber and Deborah McCarthy (eds.), *Foundations for Social Change: Critical Perspectives on Philanthropy and Popular Movements* (Rowan & Littlefield, 2005)

Karen Ferguson, *Top Down: The Ford Foundation, Black Power, and the Reinvention of Racial Liberalism* (University of Pennsylvania Press, 2013)

Arthur Hobhouse, *The Dead Hand: Addresses on the Subject of Endowments and Settlements of Property* (Chatto & Windus, 1880)

Erica Kohl-Arenas, *The Self-Help Myth: How Philanthropy Fails to Alleviate Poverty* (University of California Press, 2015)

Maribel Morey, *White Philanthropy: Carnegie Corporation's 'An American Dilemma' and the Making of a White World Order* (UNC Press Books, 2021)

J.B. Schneewind (ed.), *Giving: Western Ideas of Philanthropy* (Indiana University Press, 1996)

Edgar Villanueva, *Decolonizing Wealth: Indigenous Wisdom to Heal Divides and Restore Balance* (Berrett-Koehler, 2018)

Darren Walker, *From Generosity to Justice: A new Gospel of Wealth* (Ford Foundation, 2019)

Paul Woodruff (ed.), *The Ethics of Giving: Philosophers' Perspectives on Philanthropy* (Oxford University Press, 2018)

Philanthropy or the State?

William Beveridge, *Voluntary Action (Works of William H. Beveridge): A Report on Methods of Social Advance* (Routledge, 2014)

Maria Brenton, *The Voluntary Sector in British Social Services* (Longman, 1985)

Michael Chesterman, *Charities, Trusts, and Social Welfare* (Weidenfeld and Nicolson, 1979)

Geoffrey Finlayson, *Citizen, State, and Social Welfare in Britain, 1830–1990* (Oxford University Press, 1994)

Benjamin Kirkman Gray, *Philanthropy and the State: Or, Social Politics* (P.S. King, 1908)

Matthew Hilton and James McKay (eds.), *The Ages of Voluntarism: How We Got to the Big Society* (Oxford University Press for the British Academy, 2011)

Philanthropy or Democracy?

Beth Breeze, *In Defence of Philanthropy* (Agenda Publishing, 2021)

David Callahan, *The Givers: Wealth, Power, and Philanthropy in a new Gilded Age* (Vintage, 2017)

Linsey McGoey, *No Such Thing as a Free Gift: The Gates Foundation and the Price of Philanthropy* (Verso Books, 2015)

Rob Reich, Chiara Cordelli and Lucy Bernholz (eds.), *Philanthropy in Democratic Societies: History, Institutions, Values* (University of Chicago Press, 2016)

Rob Reich, *Just Giving: Why Philanthropy is Failing Democracy and How It Can Do Better* (Princeton University Press, 2020)

Joan Roelofs, *Foundations and Public Policy: The Mask of Pluralism* (SUNY Press, 2003)

Emma Saunders-Hastings, *Private Virtues, Public Vices: Philanthropy and Democratic Equality* (University of Chicago Press, 2022)

Philanthropy or the Market?

Matthew Bishop and Michael Green, *Philanthrocapitalism: How Giving Can Save the World* (Bloomsbury Publishing USA, 2010)

Michael Edwards, *Just Another Emperor?: The Myths and Realities of Philanthrocapitalism* (Demos, 2008)

Anand Giridharadas, *Winners Take All: The Elite Charade of Changing the World* (Penguin Random House, 2019)

Sharna Goldseker and Michael Moody, *Generation Impact: How Next Gen Donors Are Revolutionizing Giving* (John Wiley & Sons, 2020)

Peter Grant, *The Business of Giving: The Theory and Practice of Philanthropy, Grantmaking and Social Investment* (Springer, 2011)

Tyrone McKinley Freeman, *Madam C.J. Walker's Gospel of Giving: Black Women's Philanthropy during Jim Crow* (University of Illinois Press, 2020)

Sarah Roddy, Julie-Marie Strange and Bertrand Taithe, *The Charity Market and Humanitarianism in Britain, 1870–1912* (Bloomsbury Academic, 2018)

INDEX

Page numbers in *italics* refer to illustrations